Romans 8:28-29

THE
JAILHOUSE
ROCK

THE JAILHOUSE ROCK

Denny Merritt

WORD BOOKS
PUBLISHER
WACO, TEXAS

THE JAILHOUSE ROCK

All Scripture quotations, unless otherwise noted, are taken from *The Living Bible, Paraphrased* (Wheaton: Tyndale House Publishers, 1971) and are used by permission.

All Scripture marked RSV are from the Revised Standard Version of the Bible, copyrighted 1946, 1952, © 1971, 1973 by the Division of Christian Education of the National Council of the Churches of Christ in the U.S.A., and are used by permission.

Scriptures marked KJV are from the King James or Authorized Version of the Bible.

Illustrations by Phil Lester

ISBN 0-8499-2822-2
Library of Congress catalog card number: 77-92450
Printed in the United States of America

Dedicated to the Lord Jesus Christ,

my Liberator and Keeper,

and

to Jack and Berneata Merritt (Dad and Mom)

who introduced Him to me.

Contents

Acknowledgments

I want to especially thank Phil Lester for his super illustrations; Caryn Ellison, Kathy Brown, and Dave Nichols for typing the manuscripts; Dave Nichols, Ralph Hunt, Bob Laurent, and Ray Basore for proofreading, suggestions, and constant encouragement; Steve Lokker for the cover photo; Reverend Gerry Ford, his wife, Lota, and the people of Dorrisville Baptist Church for their love, generosity, and encouragement (the manuscript was written while Patty and I stayed in the Ford's cabin near Harrisburg, Illinois); my friends at Word—Gary Black, Lois Ferguson, Floyd Thatcher, Paul Van Duinen, and Margaret Walding—for sharing their hearts, talents, and resources; and finally for the love, understanding, patience, suggestions, typing and proofreading help of my partner and wife, Patty Merritt, in preparing these pages. I thank and praise God.

Introduction

When I was a kid I enjoyed playing in our big backyard, especially in the fall. By that time the frost was on the punkin', school was into its second month, and the excitement of high school football filled every ten-year-old boy's dreams. And besides all that, the grass didn't have to be mowed for nearly nine months.

Just to make sure none of the "green stuff" would survive, the guys and I trampled it under with our Monday through Friday, after-school Blooper Bowl games (we played tackle of course). If there were enough of us we'd pick captains and choose sides as wisely as we could. Sometimes that would take twenty minutes or more—after all, who wanted to go inside and face three and a half hours of television after suffering a humiliating loss on the gridiron?

When there were only seven or eight of us we'd try to choose teams by common agreement: "Let me see. We got three big kids, four medium-sized kids and a runt. That means we each get one and a half big kids (we were studying fractions at school), two medium kids and the runt's mother is calling him. Can't you hear her now? Real faint-like, 'Here, Runt, your Wheaties are ready.' Gee, tough luck, pal!"

Well, usually the team with the most big kids had it made. When I was faced with a choice of playing on a losing team from the start or not playing at all, I usually played, but not without shouts and groans of "Unfair! All we got is one scrawny ol' big kid!", or "It's a Communist plot!"

If the odds were too great against us, I quickly called the game to a halt. It was my football and my yard. And if there was one thing I hated, it was walking right into a certain loss. I faced the facts: Losing a backyard football "championship" game by the score of 60–44 wasn't my idea of a thrill, especially when the other team gave us our 44 points at the beginning just to con us into playing at all.

But once in a while the tables would turn. One night our team, the We Try Harder trio, had ferociously battled the Giants to a 12–12 tie with just a little time to go. We all knew the game was almost over because I had been called to supper nine times already. Everyone knew that the tenth call meant that the local referee (good ol' Dad) would come outside and personally put a prompt end to the contest.

We had the ball deep in our own territory. It was fourth down with nine feet to go for a touchdown. The ball was hiked to me and all my teammates (both of them) went out for a pass. The two enemy big kids covered my first teammate well because he ran a tricky pattern behind the clothesline and in between the lilac bushes. Their other man charged in after me. He was obviously out for blood—mine. I dodged him several times, but I was running out of breath—and receivers. Of course, I could always throw to my other teammate (the Runt) who was, as usual, standing still with hands pocketed in the end zone.

No one was covering him at all, but then, that was nothing new. They'd all seen him catch. And they'd seen me throw. Well, this night I was fast becoming desperate. Someone has said a tie game is like kissing your sister, and we all know how *yukky* that is.

Suddenly I heard the back door slam. Knowing that the referee was coming fast, I sidestepped the onrushing tackler one final time and unleashed the ball with all my might toward the end zone. It sailed straight through the air *perfectly*, end over end.

Since it was about three-quarters dark, and because no one had ever thrown him a pass before, the Runt never knew what hit him. The ball torpedoed into his stomach with a loud "thwump" and sent him sprawling straight backwards to the ground while he held his tummy with one hand and clutched the ball with the other. The Runt had caught the winning pass!

The referee announced that the game was over—and supper as well. We'd done it! We beat the big kids. And against overwhelming odds, too. Who cared if the Runt was now vomiting all over my new football? We won!

But since that only happened once, I normally stayed away from "lost" causes.

Nearly 1,925 years ago, a pair of praying preachers were plunged into a prison cell. They are many miles from home, imprisoned in a strange land, and nearly killed by an angry mob all because they chose up sides with a Galilean carpenter who had claimed to be the Son of God and Lord of heaven and earth. Deep in a dungeon, locked-up and forgotten, they wake up at midnight to talk and sing about Jesus, who many said made it through Roman crucifixion and death to live again.

In another part of that Philippian jail a Roman jailer, having done his duty and having the power of the state's "big guys" on his side, snoozes in peace. A couple of ragged runts are no match for a Roman prison. But, in spite of the lopsided odds and the look of certain defeat for these "Christians," it's too early to place any bets on the outcome. The game isn't over yet.

Just a few years earlier in Jerusalem, the religious "big kids" pushed through a mock trial, fixed the sides, and traded a King for a killer. Jesus of Nazareth was crucified on the town garbage heap between two thieves. It was even his tree and on his ground. It looked like God was thrown for a huge loss. But the game wasn't over. It had just begun.

Whether you're a sure winner or you think you might be a born loser, no matter what your game plan might be, pull up your stadium cushion, get your binoculars, and look back with me several hundred years. Focus in on the action. We don't want to miss a single play. Down on the field is a handful of fascinating players. One of them looks a little like you.

"And they're off!"

SENT

That night Paul had a vision. In his dream he saw a man over in Macedonia, Greece, pleading with him, "Come over here and help us." Well, that settled it. We would go to Macedonia, for we could only conclude that God was sending us to preach the Good News there (Acts 16:9–10).

We pick up the action of some key figures in the early Church, midway in Paul's second missionary journey. Silas, himself a gifted teacher and preacher, is Paul's chief companion, though young Timothy (of 1 and 2 Timothy fame) and Dr. Luke (known widely for penning the Gospel of Luke and Acts) are along much of the way. Their mission—and they decided to accept it—was to invite all who would listen to receive Jesus Christ as Lord and to encourage the converts to grow in the faith.

After receiving clear leading from the Holy Spirit not to travel to Asia or Bithynia, this group of believers went through Mysia province to the city of Troas on the coast of the Aegean Sea, where Paul experienced his vision. Now there was no doubt in his mind that God wanted the gospel preached in Macedonia. The man in the vision asked for help, and Paul knew the best kind of help available anytime could come through his risen Lord. Right away they set sail across the Aegean Sea, finally reaching Philippi, a Macedonian colony. There they stayed for several days with the first European converts—Lydia, a clothseller, and her household.

"END-COME" FACTS

The Book of Acts is really not the "acts of the apostles" nor the "acts of the early church," but the "acts of the Spirit of Jesus" through his followers. It's easy to see from the book itself that the purpose of Jesus was to spread the good news far and wide. And still today this news is so good, so startling, so life-changing, that it *has* to be shared. Jesus stated that eventually this mission would be accomplished just before his return. The command for us to "go into all the world and preach the gospel to every creature" will be fulfilled near the end of this present age: "And this gospel of the kingdom shall be preached in all the world for a witness unto all nations; and then shall the end come" (Matt. 24:14, KJV). The International Congress of World Evangelization held at Lausanne, Switzerland in 1974 had that goal in sight. We're called to be "workers together with him" to help complete the task he has begun in reaching out to a dying humanity.

GOD ALWAYS SEEKS US FIRST

None of us rightly can accuse our Creator of neglect. As God has revealed himself through the Bible and through his son Jesus we see a personal, loving God who highly values man. From the very first human pair to the present—regardless of our attitude toward him—God seeks us.

Shortly after Adam had followed Eve's suggestion and willfully disobeyed God's one negative command, we see him seeking them in the garden. This was probably the first game of hide-and-seek. Only this was no game. Their sin had brought upon them shame and guilt, and they decided to hide from God. Of course, this was impossible, but just like us today they still tried. "And they heard the voice of the Lord God walking in the garden in the cool of the day: and Adam and his wife hid themselves from the presence of the Lord God amongst the trees of the garden. And the Lord God called unto Adam, and said unto him, 'Where art thou?' " (Gen. 3:8–9, KJV). Adam and Eve were God's first two human companions, beings uniquely created in his image. But their sin brought separation and spiritual death. And they were afraid.

Yet we don't ever need to fear the one who loves us perfectly. 1 John 4:18 reminds us that "there is no fear in love; but perfect love casteth out fear: because fear hath torment. He that feareth is not made perfect in love." Sure, God could take a good look at man in his rebellion and indifference and destroy him. God could throw a couple of well-placed lightning bolts our way and roar out the warning: "It's not nice to fool Father Jehovah!" But even in his disappointment, God had a loving plan to bring "whosoever will" back to his love. Jesus would come in the form of a human "care package" and defeat Satan one day. "For God so loved the world, that he gave . . ." (John 3:16*a*).

HERE COMES JESUS

The Bible tells us that "when the fullness of the time was come, God sent forth his Son, made of a woman, made under the law, To redeem them that were under the law, that we might receive the adoption of sons" (Gal. 4:4). In other words at exactly the perfect time, Jesus came to this planet to fulfill what the Old Testament prophets had predicted. At last God's own Son had come. His purpose was to point people to his Father by inviting them to take a good, long look at himself, and especially at his death and resurrection. Through his death on the cross, Jesus paid the sin-debt for every man who would receive this gift. It's been said that *Jesus* is God spelled out in language man can understand. And the language of his great love for us is what God uses to draw us to trust him.

Jesus was the first missionary and he knew his purpose well: "For the Son of man is come to seek and to save that which was lost" (Luke 19:10). So many times the church wants to be involved in the business of "saving," but totally ignores the first task of seeking. Almost everywhere Jesus went, he walked. His journeys took him to the poor villages and homes of common sinners for which he was criticized. He walked to a well in Samaria and spoke to a misguided woman about her need for God.

> Up and down hillsides and rugged terrain,
>   through streets and alleyways,
>   on highways, by-ways,
>   cities and small villages. . . .
>
> If God became a man,
>   What would he do?
>   We know what He did.
>
> Jesus walked and sought and called people.
>   multitudes,
>   one at a time,
>   to come to him.

WE ARE "WON" IN THE SPIRIT

Jesus' public ministry on earth lasted nearly three and one-half years. Then he was crucified, buried, and God raised him from the grave. He appeared many times to the disciples and to over five hundred believers at one time. Forty days after his resurrection he ascended into heaven to be with the Father.

His physical absence from earth raises a question: Who does the job now? Who calls on people across the world to turn to God? Jesus answered that question before he left. He promised that he would send another Comforter—the Holy Spirit—to be not only with his disciples, as Jesus was, but to be in them. The Spirit of Jesus could live and work within the lives of each one who trusted in him. Through the Holy Spirit everyone, everywhere could know Jesus' nearness at the same time. Jesus would no longer be limited by a body, but the truth of his resurrection and Lordship would be launched by the Body of Christ, the Church—his people here on earth.

A revolution began at Pentecost which is destined to upset our heart's old "establishments," bringing in a brand new order. We can see Jesus alive and at work everywhere through his modern-day, Spirit-led and empowered disciples who lift up the battle-cry: POWER THROUGH THE PEOPLE! And His voice echoes in our hearts, "So send I you."

"I THOUGHT HEAVEN SENT WAS A PERFUME."

God's will and desire is that all come to repentance. It's still through his messengers today that the good news is preached and shared in the Spirit's power. The Bible speaks of men God chose or sent to be a witness. Many Old Testament prophets were commissioned from the high command. John the Baptist was sent from God (John 1:6). Sending

Ananias to lay hands on Paul following the Damascus road encounter, the Lord said, "Go and do what I say. For Paul is my chosen instrument to take my message to the nations and before kings, as well as to the people of Israel" (Acts 9:15). It was Paul who wrote the church at Corinth, "We are Christ's ambassadors. God is using us to speak to you: we beg you, as though Christ himself were here pleading with you, receive the love he offers you—be reconciled to God" (2 Cor. 5:20).

DON'T RELAX JUST YET

Some of you just said a hearty "Amen," a happy "Wow," or a thrilling "Praise the Lord!" Why? Because you think that when God sends Jesus, John the Baptist, or Paul and Silas to be his messengers, he is excluding you. I have the same problem. A few years ago I was asked to be the soloist and music director for a series of special services several miles from our home. I was thrilled to have the opportunity to be directly involved in meetings which would challenge people to give their lives to Jesus. So each afternoon I would kiss my wife, Patty, goodbye, grab my music, and head for the church. I was really bold—or so I thought. Toward the end of the week the thought began to haunt me that it sure was easy driving forty miles and shining for Jesus, but it was painfully hard to get involved with my nextdoor neighbors. Could God be telling me something in all this?

WHAT? ME WITNESS?

Jesus told his unschooled and roughshod (but redeemed!) band of disciples that they were to be witnesses about his death and resurrection to ". . . the people in Jerusalem, throughout Judea, in Samaria, and to the ends of the earth" (Acts 1:8). Notice that his instructions were not to pile into the Plymouth and drive for parts unknown, occasionally rolling down the windows to holler a "Jesus cheer" to an unsuspecting and disinterested public. He made it clear that the order was to "start at home and move to Rome." The Great Commission (today as practiced in many places it's the Great Omission) was not a special early church study on the problem of juvenile delinquency in South Caesarea. Its words spell "orders from the Chief." For any believer in any age to refuse to let his life and lips witness to the risen Lord is to rebel openly against God, deny himself deep joy and inner peace, and deprive people around him of eternal life. No excuse, shortcoming, or "private" interpretation of Scripture can let us off his "hook." After all, he taught the disciples to be fishers of men, didn't he?

SENT-SITIVE TO HIS SPIRIT

Paul and Silas were two such "men-fishers"—guys who walked very much in the Spirit (Rom. 8:4). If the Holy Spirit had told me not to go into Asia, I think I would have pouted and fumed for a few days, trying to figure out why God didn't like me anymore. Not Paul and Silas, though. Remember Paul would soon write to the Ephesians about "redeeming the time, because the days are evil" (Eph. 5:16, KJV). This pair simply shifted directions and headed north for Bithynia. Then wham-o! The Spirit of Jesus says no again. Did they write home for instructions? Did they call a special meeting of the "Bored"? No. They merely did a most sensible thing. They tried another route and this time, not prevented by the Holy Spirit, they went through Mysia province to Troas, where Paul received the call to Macedonia. Since their lives were dedicated to Jesus, Paul and Silas moved out and spoke up in faith, trusting Jesus by the Spirit to open and shut doors of service along the way. Which he did. And does.

"Hard or hardly?"

SUFFERING

One day as we were going down to the place of prayer beside the river, we met a demon-possessed slave girl who was a fortune-teller, and earned much money for her masters. She followed along behind us shouting, "These men are servants of God and they have come to tell you how to have your sins forgiven." This went on day after day until Paul, in great distress, turned and spoke to the demon within her. "I command you in the name of Jesus Christ to come out of her," he said. And instantly it left her. Her masters' hopes of wealth were now shattered; they grabbed Paul and Silas and dragged them before the judges at the marketplace. "These Jews are corrupting our city," they shouted. "They are teaching the people to do things that are against the Roman laws." A mob was quickly formed against Paul and Silas, and the judges ordered them stripped and beaten with wooden whips. Again

and again the rods slashed down across their bared backs; . . .
(Acts 16:16–23).

Paul and Silas had been in this Macedonian colony for
several days now and not a whole lot had happened by modern standards. One household had received their message
about Jesus, but things were looking pretty dim for any city-
wide meetings in the local circus stadium. Even so, the disciples suspected that God had plans for them in the area. They
suspected right.

There was a girl possessed by a demon. There is no indication she was paranoid. We are not led to believe that she was
experiencing drug-related hallucinations. She had a demon.
For several days she followed Paul and Silas around, crying
out loud about their identity and their purpose. Now Paul and
Silas were capable preachers, and they didn't need a fanfare.
Their preaching was inspired by the Holy Spirit, and this girl
was in need of deliverance. So Paul, in Jesus' name, ordered
the demon to leave her. It did. It had no choice.

The girl's masters didn't share her excitement over her
newfound freedom in Christ. As matter of fact they were quite
upset about it. They had made a lot of money from her
demonic power to tell fortunes and had hoped to make lots
more. Sensing recession and possible bankruptcy tumbling in
on them, they weren't in much of a mood to thank Paul and
Silas for being so kind to their "property." They wanted
revenge!

Dragging the pair bodily to the town judges, they made
false charges against them. Actually Paul and Silas, as citizens
of Rome, had broken no Roman law, for certainly no law
protected poor, innocent demons from eviction. But typical
humankind that they were, the good citizens of Philippi
wasted no time in forming a mob against Paul and Silas.

Without even a trial the judges ordered the two stripped and beaten with rods. Bruised, bloodied, and somewhat bewildered, we see the "chosen two" suddenly at a loss for words—or at least the strength to utter them.

WE DID GOOD, HUH?

"Of all the outrageous, unfair, ridiculous injustices ever pulled, this one takes the angelfood! Talk about a Watergate coverup! While Paul and Silas are minding God's own business, they get dragged halfway across town and are wrongly accused and beaten. There oughta be a law! Where's the Justice of the Peace? Or better yet, where was their piece of justice?"

That's how many of us react to this series of events. Or we bring up the old stand-by, "What's God doing all this time? It had better be a good one, Lord." The only problem with this reaction is that we're taking up a cause that Paul and Silas never raised. They didn't complain. Why?

God says "Praise the Lord if you are punished for doing right! Of course, you get no credit for being patient if you are beaten for doing wrong; but if you do right and suffer for it, and are patient beneath the blows, God is well pleased" (1 Pet. 2:19–20). It looks like God is far more interested in building our character than he is in preserving our beautiful bodies. Our "new nature" or "inner man" is what pleases him and lets others know he's real in our lives. Paul, Silas, and a host of other believers, right down to our day, know the value of suffering for doing right.

Paul wrote to the brothers in Corinth, "So we do not lose heart. Though our outer nature is wasting away, our inner nature is being renewed every day" (2 Cor. 4:16, RSV). To counter the boastings of some who had undermined his work there, Paul counts his sufferings as a privilege: "They say they serve Christ? But I have served him far more! (Have I gone mad to boast like this?) I have worked harder, been put in jail oftener, been whipped times without number, and faced death again and again and again" (2 Cor. 11:23). It sounds like a crazy way to increase patience, but we'd better withhold our judgment. These fellows knew something we don't know.

JESUS IS A RIOT

There's something about Jesus which doesn't allow for ho-hum reactions. There is no person who has ever lived nor any subject which has been discussed that instantly creates such a wide swing in human response. Perhaps we put up our defenses because we can't logically understand his announced purpose of dying for the sins of mankind. "So when we preach about Christ dying to save them, the Jews are offended and the Gentiles say it's all nonsense" (1 Cor. 1:23).

There's always the chance that we feel the Messiah shouldn't say anything, however true, which could cause anyone to be uneasy. We may feel that way, but Jesus said he "came not to send peace, but a sword" (Matt. 10:34b). Or there's the objection that Christianity is a bit too narrowminded. The fact remains that Jesus did claim to be the one and only, the same as the Father, the Light of the world.

What's the fun in all of that? Where's our freedom to shop around for the kind of Lord who suits our fancy? Only one Jesus? Why, that's unAmerican. What ever happened to free enterprise, healthy competition, and Horatio Alger? Isn't it against some law somewhere to have a monopoly on being the Son of God?

So in our frustrating search to be free on our own, making a Savior in our own image, we crucify and try to forget about Jesus. We ignore his book. We camouflage his story behind "ho-ho-ho" and Peter Cottontail. We close our eyes to the

world he made and holds together. We stuff cotton in both
ears and shout at the top of our lungs to drown this hopefully
insignificant Galilean out of our minds.

And quietly, from the depths of our souls, comes floating
softly and then churning madly to the surface: "And there is
salvation in no one else, for there is no other name under
heaven given among men by which we must be saved" (Acts
4:12, RSV). Jesus. You either know him and love him, or you
run from his love and his people, racing frantically from door
to door, hoping to find a more pleasant substitute—which
doesn't exist.

AIN'T IT GRAND TO BE A CHRISTIAN?

Too often we in the Church look at the way things are in our
lives and proudly suppose that this is the way things were
intended to be. For example, we read 1 Peter 2:21, "This
suffering is all part of the work God has given you. Christ,
who suffered for you, is your example. Follow in his steps."
Then we stop and think to ourselves, "This verse speaks of
suffering as being part of the work God has given me. Now,
let me see. I didn't realize that I was suffering at all. But I
must be. Oops! I mean, isn't it grand to suffer so for our
gracious Lord?" Then we start making lists of all the supposed
"crosses" we must bear as we follow in his steps. Usually we
list such hardships and burdens as regular church attendance,
midweek or special services, having to give some of our
money to support the church programs, not to mention the
times we actually steal precious seconds a day to read the
Bible and say a fleeting prayer.

Once my wife, Patty, and I lived on a dirt road nearly a
quarter of a mile from the nearest main highway. We had
attended a midweek church function one spring evening, and
it had been raining all day. When we arrived at our corner, I

discovered that the dirt road had changed into a very slushy mudslide. Knowing that our car couldn't possibly make the climb, we began trudging uphill to our home. Since we had also done laundry that afternoon, I was carrying all of our books and two bags of clothes, while Patty was walking barefoot to protect her good shoes.

A hundred yards into our pilgrimage, Patty, her feet cold and smarting, began to cry. This gave me a chance to play Denny the Martyr. Books under my arms and two heavy clothes bags over each shoulder, I bent down and carried Patty piggyback all the way up the steep grade. Did I ever feel proud of old Den! The Lord really had a trooper in me. That's for sure. What a disciple I was becoming. Sure, my back would probably require surgery, but the victory was won.

WHAT VICTORY?

Within recent years the major news services have reported widespread persecution of Christians around the world. In the African country of Chad over 130 people were crucified and buried alive simply for claiming Jesus Christ as Lord. The entire world has been stunned by the horrors in Uganda. So many are being persecuted, tortured and killed within Iron Curtain nations that it is said our generation is experiencing the most extensive persecution of Christians since the first century. I personally do not want to be tortured or to see friends or family go through persecution for any reason. However, I don't want to insult the Word of God by claiming to suffer for Jesus' sake when I really don't. Climbing up a muddy hill on a rainy spring night, my sweetie close behind me, yards from a warm house, is not suffering. Sitting in a hard pew for one hour a week is not suffering. Taking the terrible risk of someone saying, "So what?" to our well-intended "Jesus loves you" is not suffering.

The Apostle Paul wrote from personal experience the inspired advice, "Indeed all who desire to live a godly life in Christ Jesus will be persecuted" (2 Tim. 3:12, RSV). If it's true, and I believe it is, that we don't really know what it means to be persecuted as free-world believers, then perhaps we need to learn what it is to "live a godly life in Christ Jesus"—not merely to say that we too are sufferers, but to obey with all our hearts the Man who stirs the world with its false hopes to turn to him.

"There! That should take care of that!"

SECURE

And afterwards they were thrown into prison. The jailer was threatened with death if they escaped, so he took no chances, but put them into the inner dungeon and clamped their feet into the stocks (Acts 16:23b–24).

By this time in their Philippian stay, Paul and Silas were in no condition to be properly introduced to anyone. However, they were welcomed to their new quarters by their congenial host, an unnamed Roman jailer. *Thrown into prison* is probably a literal phrase here, naturally following the earlier rough treatment of the pair. And the conditions of their visit were made very plain to their keeper.

The penalty for a Roman jailer who allowed a prisoner to

escape was death. Our jailer friend, possibly a retired Roman officer, was reminded that this case was no exception. In no uncertain terms he was told, "If these jailbirds fly, you' gonna die!" This being the case our jailer wasn't pokey in securing them in his "pokey."

Faced with the possibility of his own death and warned in advance about the two "scoundrels" and their God, the jailer wisely took no chances. I wouldn't have either. He paid little attention to providing these roaming rabble-rousers with all the comforts of home, let alone Rome. When your own life is at stake no ordinary prison cell is enough distance between your captives and freedom. So the jailer tossed them into the inner dungeon of the prison—probably a damp, unventilated, rat-infested cubicle. We know for sure that it was dark. Just to make extra certain there would be no chance of an escape, he clamped their feet into the stocks. There! Now he could relax.

But he couldn't be too careful. Weren't these the two strangers who stirred the whole city into an angry mob and threatened to ruin some of the downtown businessmen? Well, they didn't look so tough now, groaning with pain and all crumpled up in the corner of the top security cell. No one had ever escaped from the inner dungeon under his protection. And these two weather-beaten preachers wouldn't be the first. No siree!

I FEEL LIKE A MILLION

Most of us don't worry about the inevitability of our own death. It's not because we're especially ready to go or because we're comfortable with thoughts of the "great beyond." We just generally block it out of our minds. Our culture is a witness to the fear which lurks within us concerning what the Bible speaks of as our "appointed time to die" and "after this the judgment."

Ours is the generation of medical discoveries which lead to a lower death rate by natural causes. America is the land "for those who think young." Isn't it only a matter of time before wild hickory nuts will prolong our lives, cure our arthritis, and bring world peace? We're not getting older, we're getting better. We can't die. There are too many plans which would be spoiled. There are plans for the new house, the expansion of our business, continuation of our education, and what about the wedding? We plan our wardrobes, tomorrow's meals, summer vacations, and we mustn't forget the next six month's worship services. We make plans for every major undertaking—except our own.

Somehow our electronic society has millions of us brainwashed into believing that it can't happen here. And just as we push the knob on our television sets and watch the little circle of light fade away into nothingness only to see it resurrected at dawn to play in newness of commercials, so also we will return—preceded, of course, by our favorite national anthem.

God's wisdom interrupts our favorite program with this bulletin: "Don't brag about your plans for tomorrow—wait and see what happens" (Prov. 27:1). In spite of our uneasiness over these words, we're a lot like the jailer. We toss the deepest questions of life into our mind's dungeon, lock 'em up tight, and carry on as usual, except for that occasional uneasy feeling that what we've been dodging must someday be faced. After all, "what makes us think that we can escape if we are indifferent to this great salvation announced by the Lord Jesus himself, and passed on to us by those who heard him speak?" (Heb. 2:3).

WHAT MAKES US THINK?

When I was in high school a serious-minded upperclassman

asked me if I had a philosophy of life. I began to expound
upon the wonders of brotherly love, the Golden Rule, the
Beatles, and other impressive ingredients. It didn't take me
long to realize that my philosophy of life was a mess. My
questioner just shook his head and walked off, leaving me
scratching mine.

The more I thought about life and the sense of it all, a great
truth began to dawn on me. What most of us think about life's
meaning is a result of how we cope daily with people, problems, and events. And in these times of "future shock"
living—in which nearly twenty-five percent of the adult,
American public is suffering from some form of mental
illness—"keeping it from falling apart" demands more of our
attention than "getting it all together."

I discovered that while I was so busy running from place to
place, plugging up holes in the dike of living, I never got
topside long enough to peak at the entire horizon. For a long
time I had it figured that there was no horizon, no sky, no
purpose, and that my dike and I just sorta happened along
accidentally. Then it came to my mind that Somebody else
had already dealt with the "why" questions—successfully. He
said things like: "Stop fooling yourselves. If you count yourself
about average in intelligence, as judged by this world's standards, you had better put this all aside and be a fool rather
than let it hold you back from the true wisdom from above.
For the wisdom of this world is foolishness to God" (1 Cor.
3:18–19). And right when I was ready to explain to him why I
disagreed with some of his methods he laid it out plain. "This
plan of mine is not what you would work out, neither are my
thoughts the same as yours! For just as the heavens are higher
than the earth, so are my ways higher than yours, and my
thoughts than yours" (Isa. 55:8–9). I began to try to figure out
what this statement meant. I had taken a seventh grade

science course in which we studied all about the universe (in two weeks), and I knew that scientists have theorized that the universe might be endless. Yet God says to me that in comparison to my understanding, his knowledge is infinitely more complex. Slowly I began to sense that he was definitely in a league all by himself. However, this was all right with me, because I didn't want to play against him anyway.

BLANKET STATEMENTS

The *Peanuts* character Linus is typical of so many of us. In his blanket is security, warmth, beauty, truth, and life itself. With his blanket, Linus is a worldbeater. Without his blanket he is like Samson without his hair, L. without his B.J., Howard Cosell with Muhammed Ali.

Many of us get all wrapped up in jobs, popularity, family concerns, romance, or success. And like Linus we ask, "Is there anything more?" The jailor of Philippi was preoccupied with survival and doing his job well. Like most of us, he didn't ask a lot of questions. His "blanket" seemed to be meeting most of his needs.

The trouble with the "blanket" way of life is that it slips away. A lot of time is spent in repairing, cleaning and protecting our various blankets. Yet millions won't admit that pulling all sorts of cumbersome blankets along through life is, in reality, a "drag." The Scriptures warn that "Before every man there lies a wide and pleasant road that seems right but ends in death" (Prov. 14:12). Most "free-ways" are deadends.

Actually the very best plan for security is an "inside job." A popular singing group in the sixties sang a tune which contained the question, "How can I be sure? In a world that's constantly changing, how can I be sure. . . ." It is this penetrating desire to know something or someone we can depend on that causes us to pile the security blankets so high. God urges each one of us to trust in his unchanging love that was demonstrated in the life of his Son, Jesus Christ, "the same yesterday, today, and forever" (Heb. 13:8).

Right this moment he's asking you to let every false prop drop from your hands as you choose to put yourself in his hands. Jesus promises to give eternal life to his own who follow him, ". . . and they shall never perish, neither shall any man pluck them out of my hand. My Father, which gave them me, is greater than all; and no man is able to pluck them out of my Father's hand." (John 10:28–29, KJV). When Jesus comes to live in our hearts by the Spirit, are we secure at last? "No one, regardless of how shrewd or well-advised he is, can stand against the Lord" (Prov. 21:30). Build a fire boys! It's blanket burning time! Then we can relax.

"Now I lay me down to sleep. . . ."

SLEEPING

Around midnight . . . the jailer wakened (Acts 16:25, 27).

After the jailer had secured Paul and Silas in the inner dungeon of the prison, he probably made other last-minute, routine checks of the compound and then returned to his quarters somewhere within the prison grounds. The text indicates that several hours had elapsed between the mock trial and the jailing, and that it was now nearly midnight.

Since we are told that a phenomenon took place which woke the jailer out of his sleep, we are to assume that he had gone to bed after a long day of activities. This was a man who was in full-time employment for the professional Roman forces and was entrusted with a post which required great responsibility on his part. His orders had been given him, and he carried them out to the letter.

No doubt he thought some about the possibility of Paul and Silas escaping from the maximum security arrangement, but each time this occurred to him he put it from his mind. By simply recalling all of his precautions to prevent the jailbreak, every fear could easily be calmed. These two prisoners had been physically dragged through town. Both of them were beaten with wooden rods—probably 39 times each. Upon arriving at the jail they were roughly dumped into the inner dungeon. And finally their feet were clamped into stocks, held fast by chains.

Perhaps as he lay back in his bed that evening, a smile slowly drew the jailer's mouth into a grin. "Certainly my prisoners and their so-called god have caused quite a stir," he thought to himself, "But for me, I see nothing to get so shook-up about." And he rolled over confidently, permitting sleep to overtake him.

"I DIDN'T HEAR A THING."

While the jailer is sleeping so soundly, let's take a look at some things which are true of us when we are physically or spiritually sleeping. Have you ever slept through a severe thunderstorm? When told of lightning illuminating the sky all around the house, terrible crashing thunder, and winds of gale force, all you could say, with some relief in your voice was, "Gee, I didn't hear a thing."

If our spiritual condition is a drowsy, self-satisfied one, we're very unlikely to tune in to the message God wants us to hear. God's plan is to communicate his love and new life to a sleepy, over-Sominexed world through his Word. We're told that "Faith cometh by hearing, and hearing by the Word of God" (Rom. 10:17, KJV). Jesus spells out just how important it is to us that we be ready to hear what he's trying to tell us: "Truly, truly, I say to you, he who hears my word and believes him who sent me, has eternal life; he does not come into judgment, but has passed from death to life" (John 5:24, RSV). The belief or trusting which leads to eternal life comes as a result of our really hearing what God is saying. Many have only casually listened to a message about Jesus and a few have even made some offhanded response. But wonderful words of life need a more careful hearing. So be careful how you listen, "For to him who has will more be given, and he will have plenty; but from him who has not, even the little he has will be taken away" (Matt. 13:12). If you're sound asleep and think you're comfy, you make it hard for his voice to get through.

F, D, P, Q, D, E, Z, R, T, O, L

When I was ten years old my parents took us on a vacation which included a trip to Carlsbad Caverns in New Mexico. Into this huge, chilly, bat-infested cave I bravely trudged, holding my Dad's hand tightly. After walking many feet underground, our tour guide wanted to give us a thrill by showing us what the word *dark* really meant. He gave the signal and one-by-one all of the lights were switched off. I squeezed Dad's hand extra tight—just in case he got scared, you understand—and thrust my other hand up to my face. I opened my eyes wide until they almost covered my forehead and still—no hand! This seemed to be carrying things a bit too far. I finally closed my eyes and pretended that the lights were really on. After what seemed an eternity, marvelous, exciting, friendly, warm light came flooding over my being, and I could see once again. My hand has never looked as good as it did that summer day.

People who are asleep don't perceive the things going on

around them either. You can place your hand in front of a sleeping person's face, and he won't even know it's there. The Scriptures teach us that there is such a thing as being asleep to the "Light of the World," God's Son. This explains why so many people, eyes wide open and aware of natural occurrences, are blind to the truth of God's plan for their lives.

The Holy Spirit made Paul aware of one reason for spiritual blindness: "If the Good News we preach is hidden to anyone, it is hidden from the one who is on the road to eternal death. Satan, who is the God of this evil world, has made him blind, unable to see the glorious light of the Gospel that is shining upon him, or to understand the amazing message we preach about the glory of Christ, who is God" (2 Cor. 4:3–4). Those who continually close themselves off from the gospel message through willfully closing their eyes are deciding to take an eternal death sentence. "Their sentence is based on this fact: that the Light from heaven came into the world, but they loved the darkness more than the Light, for their deeds were evil" (John 3:19). Millions are now spiritually asleep. Many never wake up. Will you?

REST IN PEACE

The Bible compares a man whose spirit is dead without the Holy Spirit living within, to one being asleep. "That is why God says in the Scriptures, 'Awake, O sleeper, and rise up from the dead; and Christ shall give you light' " (Eph. 5:14). Speaking to believers who had decided to live for Jesus, Paul reminded them that formerly they were dead in trespasses and sins (Eph. 2:1).

The whole world of conscious reality is closed off to the person who sleeps physically. To those who choose to remain dead and asleep by tuning out the call of Jesus to know life in all its fullness, the entire world of spiritual reality is closed.

When Jesus enters a life he makes our spirits alive so we can see and enter the kingdom of God. We can't find him in a test tube, at the end of a microscope, or by traveling to the end of our galaxy in a space capsule. But by the Spirit he enters and gives new birth to the inner space within every one of us, if we'll wake up to his gentle alarm.

You may die or he may return and you could be sadly asleep. You don't need improvement, rest, religion, or resuscitation. You need life which comes from a right relationship to Jesus. ". . . You know how late it is; time is running out. Wake up, for the coming of the Lord is nearer now than when we first believed" (Rom. 13:11). A sleepworld is a dreamworld. For those physically dead there is no time for decisions. If you're spiritually dead, there's only one to make which leads to life. Wake up to Jesus! Talk to him! Sing his song. You too can know what it really means to rest—and in peace.

"Let's just praise the Lord."

SINGING

Around midnight, as Paul and Silas were praying and singing hymns to the Lord—and the other prisoners were listening . . . (Acts 16:25).

Several hours after they were introduced to the latest in Philippian "lowrise compartments," Paul and Silas began to show signs of life. No doubt dazed for most of their early stay in the dungeon, their minds were becoming alert and they began to react in disciple-like fashion to their predicament. Here they were in Philippi with no particular place to go—all "tied up" for the moment—so they started to praise the Lord anyway.

We don't know exactly what they were praying, but it's

interesting to speculate. We know they were praying out loud, because the other prisoners were listening. It appears that the criminals down the way had no choice in the matter. They couldn't very well turn the channel. Indeed Paul and Silas had a live, captive audience. But they didn't preach; they prayed.

We're also told that along with talking to their Lord, they were actually singing hymns to him. Talk about fanatics! Here it wasn't even the Lord's Day, there was no choir loft (they were obviously an *underground* church group), no organ music was playing. After what they'd been through that very day it's hard to imagine them singing "God Is So Good" with special emphasis on the verse, "He'll set us free, he'll set us free, he'll set us free, he's so good to me," or the gospel tune "I'll Fly Away."

Paul and Silas certainly had some strange methods of reaching the townspeople. They had had some success in reaching people for Jesus "down by the riverside," but now, in the local dungeon of all places, they organize a midnight hymn-sing and gospel jamboree. And they're the only two who seem to be "getting into it."

The other prisoners were also awake, listening to the latest additions to their little family. They overheard Paul and Silas making some requests known to their God while praising him for the way things were turning out. We don't know if any prisoners ridiculed Paul and his friend, but we do know that after the prayers were answered, the convicted captives stayed captive. One thing was for sure—these new fellows were either very strange or for real. The answer was only seconds away.

KNOCK-KNOCK-KNOCKING ON HEAVEN'S DOOR

By modern standards Paul and Silas were somewhat deluded in their notions that specific prayer made to God is actually linked up with specific replies on his part. What many of us think of as laborsome drudgery, two first-century disciples considered as natural and necessary as breathing. Prayer was never intended to be the highly disciplined activity of a few hand-picked saints, preachers, and grandmas who have nothing else to do. Taking our thanks, requests, and questions to our heavenly Father is our means of keeping communication lines open with Jesus about his plan for our lives. Just as relationships on a human-to-human level must be built slowly and with consistency in love, so must our relationship with God be built as we honestly share our lives with him. Paul and Silas had led lives of prayer, so when the crisis came, "Who Can I Turn To?" was no problem with them. The normal Christian life is the life which opens itself up to God through his Word and by prayer.

Jesus said "men ought always to pray, and not faint" (Luke 18:1, KJV). Paul and Silas knew this command and the promised results from a faithful and loving Father. "Don't you think that God will surely give justice to his people who plead with him day and night?" (Luke 18:7). It's hard to know what prayers were said to God that night in a Macedonian prison cell. But knowing Paul's close relationship and deep commitment to his Savior, it's very hard to imagine him reciting a form prayer or one of our favorite creeds in hopes that God would get the message. Some churches sanction meaningless, "cookbook prayers" without even knowing it. They usually go something like this, though not nearly so brief:

> Dear Heavenly Father, we thank thee for this beautiful day which thou hast given us, and for all the many blessings which art so bountifully bestowed upon us. We ask thy special blessing on this service and on all the missionaries unable to be with us this morning. Be very near to Pastor

ah, . . . er, . . . that is, be especially with our dear Rev. oh, . . . a, . . . Well, bless the man bringing us the message this morning—thou knowest who he is, dear heavenly Father. Accept our tithes and offerings. Save the lost and don't lose the saved. And, dear heavenly Father, forgive us our many, many sins and all the places wherein we, all the time, moment-by-moment, every one of us, fail thee so miserably without fail. Oh, yes, and use us this day to thy honor and glory. In Jesus' name, Amen.

I suppose I've heard variations on this prayer hundreds of times over the years. But from the answer Paul and Silas got, it seems clear that they didn't waste time with any empty phrases of lofty-sounding words. They had confidence that God was going to see them through.

What would we have said to the Lord in that "God-forsaken" place? What did they say? No doubt the two were aware of Jesus' words about prayer for enemies. In Matthew 5:44 these directions are recorded: "Pray for those who persecute you." Their response could have been something like this:

Father of all heaven and earth, over every power and authority and demon, Satan himself, and every human being, turn those men and women around who hate Jesus so much. Reach that angry mob. Soften the hearts of those crooked judges. Convince those who beat us that their line of work isn't exactly a loving job. And Lord, touch the lives of these other prisoners. They must know their lives are in a mess. Make them see that the Lord Jesus can set them free indeed. Wake this jailer up too, Lord. We didn't get to know him at first, but he surely needs to hear the good news about new Life through your resurrection power also. He's in a key place to spread the gospel to desperate people. Save him, Lord. Send your spirit in a mighty way! We trust your perfect will, Lord.

After having called on God to work in the lives of their enemies, for whom Jesus died also, these prayer-warriors must have settled back on Jesus' promise. "And all things, whatsoever ye shall ask in prayer, believing, ye shall receive" (Matt. 21:22, KJV).

"OH, GOSH, DOROTHY!"

As a little kid *The Wizard of Oz* captivated me with its plot, characterization, and just plain fun, even though the Wicked Witch used to scare me to death. I think my favorite character in the movie was the Cowardly Lion. Instead of providing Dorothy, Toto, and the others with fierce protection, he seemed to stir everyone into new waves of fright because of his poor self-image. The irony of the whole thing left me weak with laughter every time this great big "king of beasts" got frightened over some little, mousey thing.

I can still see him standing behind a tree, twirling his tail innocently in hand, and roaring out such strong words as: "Oh, gosh, Dorothy, I couldn't. Ah, nope. Nope. Golly gee. A-yuk. A-yuk. I'm too fr-r-r-rightened. Nope. Nope. Nope."

This is the same way I picture myself and other believers sometimes when we come to God with obvious needs to be met and battles to be fought. We saunter up to him in "Cowardly Lion" fashion and our prayer is no stronger:

Dear Lord, Sir. I know you're too busy to listen to lil' ol' me, Lord, Sir. But as long as I've interrupted you, do you think you could give me a listen? Do ya', huh? The devil is bein' a meaney again and do you think there's any chance of your gettin' after him for me. Now I know you're busy and I'll understand if you can't help me out. After all, I'm only one of those worms that Jesus, your Son and my Hero, died on the cross for. I'm a real nothin'. Yessiree. Mr. Nothin' Believer, that's me. And you can be sure of one thing, dear Father, Sir, that if you ever need me in your Salvation Army, you can't get 'Nothin' for something. Well, I've taken up nearly eleven and three-fourths seconds of your eternal time now, so purty-please, if it be thy will to be sure, if you could help, I'd appreciate it. Goodnight, Amen, and A–yuk.

Somehow I can't see Paul and Silas at this or any point of their lives beatin' around the bush—especially when it's a burning bush. Knowing that their sins had been paid for by Jesus' death, and their lives were "hid in Christ with God," and in the Spirit they were "Seated in the heavenly places with Christ Jesus," they walked, talked and prayed like it. "And this is the confidence that we have in him, that, if we ask any thing according to his will, he heareth us: And if we know that he hears us, whatsoever we ask, we know that we have the petitions that we desired of him" (1 John 5:14–15, KJV).

Having God's promise to be heard and taken care of by him, what was stopping them from getting right down to the nitty-gritty instead of the "tutti-frutti" like so many of us do? As sons of God through Jesus Christ's resurrected life within them, they could have prayed like this:

> Father, I want to thank you for all you're doing in our lives right now. Thank you for saving and freeing that demon-possessed girl earlier today. We ask right now that you keep Satan and his forces under control and that the enemy would not be able to mess up your plans for this prison experience. Thank you for the privilege of suffering for the cause of Jesus and show us your purpose in all of this. Who do you want to hear the Good News next? Who can we share with? Lord God, either bring them to us, or shake this place down and take us to them. Thank you that what we're asking now is heard in heaven. We're under the authority of the Lord Jesus, and we make these requests in his name and under his authority.

I don't even know if they said, "Amen." We often say that word to mean, "That's all, folks" or "Sargent Bilko, over and out." When prayer is like breathing—as it was to Paul and

Silas—it's more likely they said something like, "To be continued," or perhaps they said nothing at all. One thing was for
certain, they prayed great prayers and received great answers
which shook the world. "Let us therefore come boldly unto
the throne of grace, that we may obtain mercy, and find grace
to help in time of need" (Heb. 4:16, KJV).

I'D LIKE TO TEACH THE WORLD TO SING

In recent years there has been an explosion of new songs to
praise to Jesus. The slumbering church has become the singing church under the inspired leadership of committed Christian composers, arrangers, singers, and musicians. Millions of
believers the world over have discovered that while hymns
still carry deep truths in age-old tunes, today's world also
needs and appreciates new music forms and unadorned lyrics
to take the good news of Jesus and "pass it on."

Paul and Silas lived long before even our trusted hymns
were published, yet the early Church also had ways of express-
ing their thanks and love to God through music. It was Paul
who said that the gift of Jesus couldn't be adequately ex-
plained with human wisdon. He wrote, "Thanks be to God for
his unspeakable gift" (2 Cor. 9:15, KJV).

To the growing believers in Ephesus, Paul must have
sounded like an overeager minister of music: "Talk with each
other much about the Lord, quoting psalms and hymns and
singing sacred songs, making music in your hearts to the
Lord" (Eph. 5:19). In this wise counsel we see the key to
singing directly to God. To sing in a dark dungeon at midnight
and mean it, lets us know that Paul and Silas were truly
singing "from their hearts."

THANK YOU, LORD!

Paul and Silas could sing because they practiced what God

led them to preach. I'm sure that in calling on the Lord to come to their rescue, Paul had "with thanksgiving, let [his] requests be made known unto God" (Phil. 4:6, KJV). The Bible makes it plain that the routine giving of "thanks for the grub" is merely scratching the surface in reflecting our gratefulness to the Lord. Since Jesus met our deepest human need of forgiveness which comes our way as his followers. Because "when we were yet sinners, Christ died for us" we can thank him all the time, no matter how things may appear on the surface.

The Christian life is to be lived as a grateful, loving response to Jesus who gave his life for us. The motive, thrust and meaning of discipleship springs from a thankful heart. "We love him, because he first loved us" (1 John 4:19, KJV). Paul and Silas knew abundant and eternal life through Jesus, so it was simple for these suffering saints to give thanks "always for all things unto God and the Father in the name of our Lord Jesus Christ" (Eph. 5:20, KJV). They gave thanks because they were thankful. They thanked God then having seen his love and care many times before. Today, as well, we need to "in everything give thanks: for this is the will of God in Christ Jesus concerning you" (1 Thess. 5:18, KJV).

ONLY TRUST HIM

Paul and Silas sang hymns to God and prayed because they "knew whom they believed and were persuaded that he was able to keep that which they'd committed unto him until that Day." The message of the Scriptures and the Savior, as well as the countless testimonies of modern-day witnesses to the resurrection, is that God can be trusted—for the biggest things, for the smallest things. "Putting your hand in the hand of the Man from Galilee" is smart.

Many have said that religion is a crutch. I won't quibble

with that. Plain old, dusty, dried-up, dead religion—religion
that doesn't point people to a relationship with a risen, return-
ing Savior—is a crutch. But it's a crutch which won't hold
anybody up because it's phony. Everyone who has ever
been born into this human race has needed all the healing,
stability, and help he could get to walk this path of life in the
manner God intended him to. But Jesus is the only crutch
who'll keep you from falling away from God to a real place
called "hell."

Jesus isn't just a crutch, though. He's your legs so you can
walk with him, your life so you can live forever with him, your
wings so you'll be able to fly up to meet him when he comes.
Jesus is even the way to travel.

Around the world there are many who still reject Jesus, and
yet they don't have a leg to stand on. They say, "I don't need
any crutches like that. I'm doing fine." But they're lost,
stumbling, and falling without the Lord as their foundation.

It's sad when a man stiffens his neck toward God and, in his
weakness and rebellion, screams, "I'm doing my own thing,
God. I don't need you." It's like a person drowning, bobbing
up and down in the water before going under for the third and
last time. Though help is all around the second time to the
surface, he yells madly, "Get away from me. I want my
freedom to do my own thing. I'm doing just fine by myself.
Can't you see I don't need anyone to do my swimming for
me?" And after sinking to the depths, he fights wildly to the
top once more. The lifeguard pleads with him to be saved and
quit fighting the inevitable, that without help he's doomed.
But there's no convincing this proud man: "Others might
need your help, lifeguard, but not me. I'll show you. I'll show
everybody. I'm a self-made man, so thanks, but no thanks.
Don't I look like I'm able to save myself. Look at me. Just look
at me!" And down to his death he sinks.

God gives all of us, because of his respect for our free will, the choice of going it alone or being towed to victory and safety through the power of the eternal lifeguard, Jesus Christ.

Shortly before going to sleep that night, our jailer friend had cause to feel pretty self-sufficient. But to all of us who think we're pulling one over on the Creator, we can stop fooling ourselves. He's got us pegged. "I know you well—you are neither hot nor cold; I wish you were one or the other! But since you are merely lukewarm, I will spit you out of my mouth! You say, 'I am rich with everything I want; I don't need a thing!' And you don't realize that spiritually you are wretched and miserable and poor and blind and naked" (Rev. 3:15–17). Since he knows us so very well and still sent his Son to take our sin penalty, his love for us is even more amazing. God, above anyone else, can be trusted.

He Has Overcome

We have no indication that the hymns our "heroes of the faith" sang while in prison were funeral dirges. From Paul's writings there is no evidence that Christians are to sound, look, or act mournful—ever. "Rejoice in the Lord alway: and again I say, Rejoice" calls out the Apostle (Phil. 4:4, KJV). The power of praise is not a twentieth-century invention, but a rediscovery of another side of the normal Christian life.

Paul and Silas had been dispatched as representatives of King Jesus, they were strangers and aliens in a foreign land, and they knew that their business was done in the name of a conquering ruler. "He disarmed the principalities and powers and made a public example of them, triumphing over them in him" (Col. 2:15, RSV). This Jesus who so powerfully broke into Paul's life on a business trip to Damascus is not just a carpenter who happened to say a few niceties and then check out

of the world. He's not just another philosopher who added a
few words of wisdom to Paul's already overflowing
storehouse. Jesus was of far greater stature than merely to
give these preachers a few more sermon illustrations. Jesus is
the sermon. "All things were created through him and for
him" (Col. 1:16b, RSV).

We shouldn't get so astounded that the first thoughts of the
waking prisoners would be of their Lord. He was there, and
they knew if they would couple their faith to his power, the
victory in this situation would be shown to them. "For whatsoever is born of God overcometh the world: and this is the
victory that overcometh the world, even our faith" (1 John
5:4, KJV). They had been fearless and faithful. It was God's
move.

"Jailhouse Rock"

SHAKEN

Around midnight, as Paul and Silas were praying and sing-ing hymns to the Lord—and the other prisoners were listening—suddenly there was a great earthquake; the prison was shaken to its foundations, all the doors flew open—and the chains of every prisoner fell off! (Acts 16:25–26).

We aren't told exactly how long Paul and Silas held their watchnight prayer service. Nor do we know if this occurred on the regular midweek church night. We're simply told that the hour was approaching midnight with the itinerant ministerial alliance singing hymns to God and praying as well. We're not given precisely what their requests were either, although we have a pretty good idea from what happened to dismiss their service. Right in the middle of what seemed like a moonlight serenade to the other prisoners, it struck, and the world seemed to cave in.

Luke's description doesn't miss a trick: "Suddenly there was a great earthquake." If there's one thing God's Word can't be accused of, it's the exaggeration or whitewashing of an event. You or I might toss adjectives around like they were meaningless words—*fantastic*, *stupendous*, *colossal*, *super*, *outa sight*—but the Holy Spirit-inspired writers didn't. Luke said it was a "great" earthquake. Why was it so great?

Three things happened in a matter of seconds which would make any self-respecting seismologist take notice. First, the prison was shaken to its foundations. An intelligent observer, learning of a fairly strong earthquake striking near the prison could easily understand this. Earthquakes occur when pressures in the earth cause movements in the crust along an already weak spot called a "fault." Foundations of buildings are anchored underground therefore, we might expect the prison's foundations to shake noticeably. Next, we're told "all the doors flew open." This earthquake is suddenly hoisted into the "very good" category, but we still might expect this, after all, strong Roman locks cannot hold out the power of an earthquake. However, considering these two phenomena plus one other qualifies our earthquake as "great" indeed.

The record is very clear at this final point: " . . . the chains of every prisoner fell off." Now this dramatic event pushes the earthmoving act into the Great Earthquake Division. The chains weren't yanked from the wall and left dangling from the prisoners. No, the Bible indicates that the chains of every prisoner fell off—off the prisoners. Now considering that fact, we just might call this event a miracle. In fact, it had to be. What you might call a "righteous rumble." It was all God's "fault." Of course, if you feel uncomfortable considering accounts of miracles, it's possible that you don't know the all-

powerful creator God, because it's basic to his nature that
everything he does is miraculous by our standards. Paul and
Silas didn't let the whole thing get them down. They knew a
great earthquake when they felt one. They also knew a great
God.

Make the World Go Away

This is not an easy generation to cope with. Pressures and
tensions are mounting daily, threatening to end all meaningful life aboard Spaceship Earth. As man has advanced
technologically, materially, and educationally, worldwide
problems have advanced also. Alongside discoveries in
medicine and industry have come biological warfare and
thermonuclear weapons capable of killing every human being
on the globe a hundred times over. The rich get richer and
the poor get poorer. But many of the poor are beginning to
catch on.

The hiking of Middle East oil prices as well as the sky-
rocketing prices of many other natural commodities from
lesser-developed countries is causing the world money flow
to reverse itself drastically. Because of the vast economic in-
terdependence which now exists in the world, worldwide
depression has again been talked about as a real threat.
World-tarnishing water, air, and land pollution continue to
take their toll, though some efforts to curb the tide are successful. Overpopulation in underdeveloped nations, coupled
with poor agricultural resources and the free world's inability
to do the job, is making this the generation of worldwide
famine.

Electronic media speed the unwelcome news to us every
hour on the hour of "wars and rumors of wars" in many places
at once. Plunging headlong at future-shock speed toward the
century mark, our global village is desperate for confident,

capable leadership. Doomsday is predicted by politicians, biologists, population experts, and atomic scientists.

Paul talked about God's creation "groaning" and "waiting patiently and hopefully for that future day when God will resurrect his children" (Rom. 8:19). Hope seems to be a rapidly dwindling commodity in a world where men and nations are falling down.

MY COUNTRY 'TIS OF THEE

The bicentennial celebration of a great nation normally breeds pride, patriotism, and a deep sense of achievement and hallowed traditions. Not so with the United States of America. Somehow, we've let the golden age slip past us. All of a sudden the invincible from without has become the undermined from within. No longer can it be said that we're untouched by the greed, lust for power, and social unrest of a technological age.

Within the last several years the man on the street has been jolted by the American Nightmare, instead of called forward to respond to the American Dream. The lethargic decade of the fifties is way behind us. The times, they are a 'changin'. The assassinations of President Kennedy, Martin Luther King, Jr., and Robert Kennedy sent wave upon wave of shock the world over. The nation's people, trying to discover if man can be truly free even in a democracy, have been catapulted from one rights conflict to another. Blacks, women, students, Chicanos, Indians, and various other groups within our society have fought against the "establishment" in search of economic, educational, and social equality.

None of this has occurred without violence, hatred, and bitterness. The nation whose founders had sought to establish a country "under God, indivisible" is still reeling from the effects of "God-is-dead" theology and years of "rebels with causes." Our children have been taught in public schools that this nation seldom if ever makes mistakes in foreign policy, and yet the recent past seems to contradict that. The American public suspects that it's often been lied to by its leaders. The seemingly endless years of Vietnam—costing thousands of American lives, ruining countless others, and spending billions of dollars—brought the spirit of '76 to an all-time low. The Watergate affair—the mess, the press, the cover-up, and the agony—all but dealt a deathblow to confidence in our national leadership, especially the Presidency.

In recent years, inflation leading to recession has threatened that prize bulwark of American life, freedom, and optimism—the dollar. Hundreds of thousands are bankrupt, with millions on the unemployment rolls. We are experiencing energy crisis, economic crisis, leadership crisis, and world respect crisis. If John Q. Public ever needed unwavering security from the "land of the free and the home of the brave" he does now. That security, however, seems unlikely to develop for there's another far more serious crisis coming which people of every nation around the world must face—it's called "tomorrow."

The "Great" Society

The earthquake which shook the Philippian jail was mild compared to the tremors which are currently shaking the societies of modern man. Hailed still as having the highest standard of living ever known to man, the people of this country are rightly being jarred awake to the truth that we've expected more from the standard, but we're not getting it.

In an age when world and national pressures are bearing down on us as never before, the building block of society—the family—is coming apart at the seams. Nearly one in two marriages now ends in divorce. Roughly seventy-five percent of teenage marriages break up. Untold numbers of couples are simply living together, skipping the so-called "unnecessary formality" of matrimony. Fractured family tales, once a rare and lamented thing within our culture, now sound like the norm. Locating an unbroken home is not yet as rare as a virgin bride, but may approach those proportions in years to come. With marriages breaking down, both spouses working, and the permissive ethic leading to a breakdown of discipline within the home, runaways among teenagers have reached great numbers.

Alcoholism and other forms of drug abuse have infected great numbers of our youth and adult population. Doctors have declared venereal disease to be of epidemic proportions in our country, and still on the increase. Premarital sex, once well on the way to becoming a norm of American youth, has fully arrived. Although there are fewer unwanted pregnancies—which seems to be an encouraging sign— premarital birth control use and abortions are at new record levels.

Violent crime jumped one hundred twenty-two percent in the United States between 1960 and 1970 and is getting higher each year. Due to the mobile nature of our society, individual and family commitment to cities, states, and persons is producing a nation of migrants. Alvin Toffler, in his widely-known book, *Future Shock*, says our fast-paced, technological, urban-centered culture causes us to make shallow, short-term relationships with "throw-away people." Our government announces plans to know us as a multi-digit number, as does West Germany with its citizens now. If we weren't already in a stupor we might be shaken a bit. Surely the bridges are burning around us. And the waters are troubled. Through the wasteland of our world we can barely make out the calm, reassuring voice of One who promises to show us the eye of the hurricane, and someday takeover: "I will never, never fail you nor forsake you" (Heb. 13:5). That announcement didn't come from God's press secretary, and he's not running for office. But we're not quite ready to give him our full, personal attention—yet.

M-M-ME? SII-SH-SH-A-A-A-K-K-K-Y-Y-Y?

Even if you've never taken a sociology or psychology course, all of you would agree that an unstable world, country, and society tend to produce unstable individuals. It's also true in reverse, that unstable individuals make up weak families, declining nations, and a teetering world. No matter which came first, the rotten egg or the fowl, pressures on us all have intensified. Never in modern history has there been such a wholesale rush by educated man to find meaning, purpose, and strength for his everyday life. Seeing that the world of science doesn't offer (and never claimed to) answers to life's most probing questions, thousands are seeking basic answers in astrology, the occult, Satan worship, Zen Buddhism, Bahai, mediumistic practices, Eastern religions, and many pseudo-Christian cults. Many still attend "weakly" worship services with little effect upon their lives, ". . . having a form of godliness, but denying the power thereof "(2 Tim. 3:5, KJV).

In our highly technologized societies, stress works itself out in our lives in a variety of ways. Some people suffer physically or psychologically, while the Bible says all suffer spiritually. Jesus sees us in our stress and invites us to know him: "Come to me and I will give you rest—all of you who work so hard beneath a heavy yoke. Wear my yoke—for it fits perfectly— and let me teach you; for I am gentle and humble, and you shall find rest for your souls; for I give you only light burdens" (Matt. 11:28–30).

Millions, however, wearily seek temporary escape from life's harsh realities. Literature, movies, television, drugs, and burying one's self in work are several means of escape. These kinds of activities eventually take their toll upon us. Dr. Nelson L. Kline, Director of Research for the Rockefeller State Research Center in Orangeburg, New York, publicly released his findings about a health menace of epidemic proportions. The disease, called "anhedonia," results in an individual being completely unable to experience pleasure of any kind. The lethargic housewife, dissatisfied businessman, and the underachieving student may well be suffering from this illness, Kline concludes.

The Bible speaks of those who have "given themselves over to sensuality, for the practice of every kind of impurity with greediness." Indicating a similarity between the modern "anhedonia" and this condition, Ephesians 4:19 refers to individuals who have hardened their hearts to God as being "past feeling." Research supporting his pronouncements, Dr. Kline says this illness now affects over twenty million Americans.

Current pressures on us bring problems which have created a boom in the number of practicing psychologists and counselors. Regardless of the fact that Vallium, a tranquilizer, is our number-one-selling drug, and Darvon, a pain killer, runs a close second, each individual has three needs which only Jesus claims to fulfill.

Jesus draws people around the world to find forgiveness, security, and purpose in him. What kind of quake would it take to wake you? Thousands in this generation from every nation are waking up to true strength, purpose, and personhood through Jesus. "This I declare, that he alone is my refuge, my place of safety; he is my God, and I am trusting him" (Ps. 91:2). Surrendered lives—they are convincing evidence!

"The Living End"

SUICIDE

The jailer wakened to see the prison doors wide open, and assuming the prisoners had escaped, he drew his sword to kill himself (Acts 16:27).

It was the midnight hour in the Philippian jail and, as the jailer "sprang from his bed to see what was the matter," he must have thought it was the end of his days rather than the beginning of a new day. After securing the compound for the night he had settled down for a well-deserved rest and had gone to sleep. But, a few hours into the night, a thundering, heavenly alarm clock in the form of an earthquake got his attention. The verse tells us simply that "the jailer wakened." That's one point for the jailer! I would have been very con-

cerned about him if he had stayed asleep during all of the
ruckus. I guess he could have stirred momentarily, decided it
was just a bunch of "Texas mice" and gone back to sleep. But
he didn't. He woke up, and "what to his wondering eyes did
appear. . . ."

The jailer probably jumped up from his sleep soon after the
quake started, and as soon as walking was safe, made his way
down to the prisoners' quarters. The sight that left his eyes
open wide was prison doors wide open—all of them. That
awful scene could only mean one thing: a "cell-out" crowd.
The prisoners must have escaped, including those two Jesus
freaks who had kept on raving about their wonderful God.
Maybe He had something to do with everything that happened. There was something a little bit unusual about those
two stirring up the town like that. Well, it didn't matter now.
They were all gone and he was a goner.

Things were too quiet in the prison. As the jailer pulled his
sword from its sheath, the noise of it no doubt filled the empty
hallway. What thoughts filled his brain? "All of those prisoners have escaped into the city of Philippi. Murderers, thieves,
scoundrels, and runaway slaves will ravage many innocent
people. The townspeople will never forgive me. All the years
I've faithfully served Rome with never a mark against me, but
now I've let an entire prison slip through my fingers. I know it
all has to do with that new God Paul and his partner Silas
seem to know so much about. He's out to get me for throwing
them in the dungeon. Well, he's got me now. Rather than let
the state executioners kill me, I'll fall on my sword. I don't
know how my family will make it, but they'll know this is the
only way. I feel so helpless. I sure didn't think my life would
end like this. Oh God of Paul and Silas, at least let me die in
peace!"

I'M ONLY HUMAN

The spring of my junior year in college was the high point of my college career, or so I thought. I had just transferred to another school, was well on the way to completing my degree in English, and was making my best grades ever. And to make everything just perfect, I had met the girl in my life who would later in the year become my wife. I was in love. I was brilliant. I was popular. And in a matter of a few years I could easily be wealthy, as my plans at the time were to graduate, go on to law school, and settle down to the business of becoming successful.

I sat back in my desk chair and pondered my life, imagining the course of events until the time I would die, with no pain and from natural causes, of course. In my "vision" I saw a stately gentleman of seventy-five years stepping out of his spacious six-bedroom house, walking out to his four-car garage, and trying to decide which of his five cars to drive to one of his three deluxe downtown offices. There I was, a successful corporate lawyer, a respected family man, and a financial whiz, just sitting around, waiting to die, and looking back.

That was the very best picture of the American Dream that my vivid imagination could put together. Wasn't that what life was all about? Wealthy, influential, successful, "professionally achieved"? In the quiet of my room, alone with my honest thoughts and desires, I gazed at my life as I had it planned and muttered to myself, "Big deal!" And the words, "What's it all about, Denny?" haunted me to alertness. Could I be missing out on something—something more? It sounded strangely familiar, like I had heard it all before:

> Beware! Don't always be wishing for what you don't have.
> For real life and real living are not related to how rich we are.

Then [Jesus] gave an illustration: "A rich man had a fertile farm that produced fine crops. In fact, his barns were full to over-flowing—he couldn't get everything in. He thought about his problem, and finally exclaimed, 'I know—I'll tear down my barns and build bigger ones! Then I'll have room enough. And I'll sit back and say to myself, "Friend, you have enough stored away for years to come. Now take it easy! Wine, women, and song for you!" ' "But God said to him, 'Fool! Tonight you die. Then who will get it all?' Yes, every man is a fool who gets rich on earth but not in heaven" (Luke 12:15–21).

HE THOUGHT HIS BODY WAS HIS SOUL

Here in black and white, from Jesus' own account, was a description of the man I was setting out to become. And God said this rich man was a fool on at least three counts. Genesis 2:7 (KJV) records that "the Lord God formed man of the dust of the ground, and breathed into his nostrils the breath of life: and man became a living soul." The Bible says that the one factor which makes man different from all of creation is that he was formed in the image of God.

As originally created, man had a body, a mind, and a spirit all of which were alive and functioning. Through Adam's willful disobedience toward God, his spirit died and each one of us is born into the world spiritually dead. When God sent the Son to be our sin-substitute, making it possible for us to know God through the Spirit, man could become whole again. Jesus said, "God is a Spirit: and they that worship him must worship him in spirit and in truth" (John 4:24, KJV). Our search to find something to fill that empty place in our spirits is, in reality, a search for the life of God. And though Jesus said in earnest that we "must be born from above" to see the kingdom of God, many still choose to live in darkness and remain the walking dead.

In trying to satisfy his emptiness the rich man Jesus talked about was looking for things. He said to himself, "Friend, you have enough stored away for years to come. Now take it easy! Wine, women and song for you!" Sitting on top of his world, this humpty dumpty didn't realize how broken up inside he really was. Seeking to find a life of meaning for his spirit, he stopped off short by planning only for physical pleasures.

I used to think God's Word was out of date, remote, and irrelevant to life today. Everywhere I turned well-meaning church people were angelically harping on the evils and ruination of this or that. But it didn't make sense to me that millions of people would smoke, drink, chew and run around if there wasn't any fun in it all. There had to be something more to sin than just the sheer enjoyment of "doing what you're not supposed to do."

Then I made a brilliant discovery: Hebrews 11:25. It told me there was pleasure in sin, "but for a season." I realized that God isn't dumb; in fact, he's really with it. He won't try to tell anyone that there isn't some temporary, physical pleasure in sin. But he makes it very plain that this pleasure won't last; and if it won't last, it doesn't satisfy.

Satan is a very crooked politician. He promises meaning and fulfillment, but the other side of his "freedom" is moral slavery and destructive habits. We swallow his talk about self-reliance and security, and he leaves us cowering inside because life is confusing and death is terrifying. We want so much to believe his talk about a new golden age for mankind, but as Armageddon looms into view we realize that we're the same, old people. His advertising men do a good job convincing us that the more we own the happier we are, yet we have this gnawing feeling that the best things in life aren't really things at all. But we constantly reelect the evil one—by choice or by apathy—to make our decisions for us.

Yes, "there is a way which seems right to a man, but its end is the way to death" (Prov. 14:12, RSV). Temporary stopgaps of sensual pleasure at the expense of true humanity through God are terribly wasteful. Our souls will spend eternity somewhere—either alive by God's power through faith or dead by our choice in hell. Your body for your soul—what kind of trade is that? "And how does a man benefit if he gains the whole world and loses his soul in the process? For is anything worth more than his soul?" (Mark 8:36–37).

DOES ANYBODY REALLY KNOW WHAT TIME IT IS?

I suppose if my folks hadn't decided to give me *Jay* as a middle name, they would have called me Denny "Procrastination" Merritt. I have been such an expert on the subject that some people think I should have been known as just plain "Pro." My greatest temptation to put off completing a task was in the area of homework. Every weekend I'd cart off every book from every class and pile them up in my room. Always wanting to do better I'd promise myself, and my parents, that this would be the weekend of the "new me," that finally I would turn over a new leaf. But as Sunday night arrived the new leaf always disintegrated into an old laugh. Halfway through "Mission Impossible" the awful truth dawned on me that I'd blown it again, and I felt like self-destructing in five seconds. The inevitable had happened. The past was gone to me, the hopeful and rewarding future had slipped behind me, and the present offered too many more pleasant distractions.

Shunning homework or house chores is a problem, but when this error in thinking invades an entire life, we make the mistake of confusing our brief lifetime with eternity. In considering his good fortune, the rich fool felt secure in that he had enough stored away "for years to come." No doubt he had been enjoying good health for sometime, and if he had enemies nearby, they didn't seem to pose any serious threat.

Therefore, since the land he tilled produced great harvests, he was counting on living for many more years.

Truthfully, all of us are like this man to some extent. The great human paradox is that most of us don't want to live and grow old, but the only other choice is to die young and we don't want that either. So we say, "Today is the first day of the rest of our lives," hardly noticing the other side of that: "Today is the last day of the first of our lives." Even though it's more common to speak of *living* another day, the truth is that we're actually one day closer to death.

Unless a prolonged illness or state of war arouses our expectations of death, it's safe to say that very few of us plan to die the day before we do. God tells us, "It is appointed unto men once to die, but after this the judgment" (Heb. 9:27). In other words, God with his foreknowledge already knows the day and hour of my death. That thought used to bug me—that God knew when I would die and wouldn't tell me. Just think how useful that information would be. But as I thought about it, if I knew exactly when, how, and where I was going to die, such knowledge would probably cause me to live each day in constant fear and avoidance of that moment, only to face the inevitable anyway.

We don't know when, but the fact remains that there is a time when we'll be clinically and actually dead and our souls will leave our bodies. "For what is your life? It is even a vapour, that appeareth for a little time and then vanisheth away" (James 4:14). Our years are few in comparison with a God who is not limited by time and space, both of which he created.

The most dangerous decision is the decision not to make a decision about who we want Jesus to become in our lives. If we ever do anything it has to be done in the present moment. Yesterday is gone. Tomorrow may or may not find us alive, but even if it does, by that time today is upon us again.

We are left with today only. We are so prone to imagine what life might be like tomorrow, or what it would have been like yesterday if only . . . , and we never come to grips with our present lives. Do we know real love, inner peace, and lasting purpose today? Do you know Jesus personally now? "Now is the accepted time; behold, now is the day of salvation" (2 Cor. 6:2, KJV).

"I" TROUBLE

In Shakespeare's tragedy *Julius Caesar*, the noble Brutus is given this sound picture of the human condition: "The fault, dear Brutus, is not in our stars, But in ourselves, that we are underlings" (Act 1, scene 1). That's a fancy way of saying what the author of the comic strip *Pogo* concluded also: "We have met the enemy and he is us." The most vicious and subtle choice of all is to confuse ourselves with God. This rich farmer had "I" trouble. In just three, short sentences he used the personal pronouns *I*, *me*, *my*, or *myself* thirteen times. There's no mention of God at all. He's stuck on himself. He's what we refer to nowadays as "into his own thing." Really that's just a nice way of saying, "He's a conceited, self-centered, self-satisfied, egomaniac off on his own trip. So don't rock his boat by telling him he's sinking fast, or he'll splash water all over you." You can catch him walking over his land, counting his money, singing his favorite song of praise, "I'm Everything to Me."

Existentialism is the modern-day disguise of this Satanic trick of letting ourselves become our own God. Made popular by Ayn Rand, Albert Camus, and others, this madness says that every man is a law unto himself. He should flaunt every standard; There is no God except himself.

But the facts of crippled and declining humanity cry out that our need to know and love "the God who is there" can never be met through prideful self-love. Countless people insist on remaining "practical atheists" by living as though God didn't exist. And it's when we stubbornly refuse to let God be God in our lives that we choose to spit on his love and welcome his judgment. "But God shows his anger from heaven against all sinful, evil men who push away the truth from them. For the truth about God is known to them instinctively; God has put this knowledge in their hearts. Since earliest times men have seen the earth and sky and all God made, and have known of his existence and great eternal power. So they will have no excuse [when they stand before God at Judgment Day]" (Rom. 1:18–20).

Everyone becomes aware of God's existence and can know him through Jesus. But we must be humble. This doesn't mean mechanically throwing ourselves face downward in the dirt and screaming and hollering for mercy. It means sincerely trying to know who God really is and who we are. The wise response is to agree with him about our condition, turn from aloneness, and receive his love and presence.

Sometimes circumstances cause us to take a fresh look at our lives. God can get through to us in many ways—through his Word, a book, sermon, friend, teacher, or even when we're by ourselves. We begin to become wise, by God's analysis, when we recognize our weakness, mortality, and sinful condition before him. And when we invite Jesus to enter our lives we receive his strength, eternal life, and are declared "not guilty" in God's eyes.

The farmer died suddenly, a fool. When will you "wise up"? It took the jailer most of his life. Then late one night, the message got through.

GOODBYE, CRUEL WORLD

The Philippian jailer was not at the point of taking his own

life. In a few brief minutes his entire world literally crumbled
to nothing while he watched. After years of indifference to the
living God he became quickly aware of his inability to please
the God of his prisoners. He was used to being in command of
his own life, planning on "many years to come," but now the
end wasn't only near, it was here.

Nearly twenty-one thousand people from a variety of occu-
pations and age levels commit suicide in this country each
year and the number is rising. Suicide is the second-leading
cause of death among people under twenty-five years of age.
To most suicide victims, the present moment is unbearable to
the point of being inescapable. Unable to retreat into a past
which brings memories of guilt, frustration, and failure, the
victims cannot stand to move into a future which holds no
hope or meaning. The vise-grips of past and future squeezing
in upon the person drive him to end it all.

The jailer was instantly thrust into this sort of situation.
What good was his past training now? And what amount of
pleading would satisfy his superiors tomorrow? Suicide was
his only escape.

Today millions, convinced that there is no alternative to
nothingness, commit slow suicide. They are too caught up in
their various forms of self-destruction disguised as "gusto" to
answer the only invitation to life. Before you decide to jump,
think about his offer of past forgiveness, present purpose, and
future security. Surely that is a better way!

"With no particular place to go."

STAYING

But Paul yelled to him, "Don't do it! We are all here (Acts 16:28).

Paul and Silas must have been thrilled to see the Lord work so convincingly in answer to their prayers. While yet in their prison cell, they became aware of the jailer's predicament. They knew the Roman laws which demanded the death penalty for sleeping on duty or allowing prisoners to escape. Either in hearing the jailer remove his sword, through common sense, or by special knowledge from God, Paul knew that the jailer was now on the brink of suicide.

The disciples could have flown the coop and been gone by this time. But they decided not to take any independent action without hearing from the Lord first, so they waited. Even after being treated with such contempt and hatred they stayed. They would have been justified in many courts of law had they murdered this jailer in self-defense and escaped. But someone in this crackerbox was ready to respond to Jesus, and they were beginning to have an idea who he might be.

When no hope was left for the jailer, Paul yelled out, "Don't do it! We are all here." Not only had the preachers stayed behind, but every other prisoner as well. For two sold-out men of God to stay put and preach the gospel might not be such a shock, but for a diversified bunch of convicts to remain quiet and contained with no chains to bind them and no doors to stop them was highly unusual. They'd heard all the singing and praying, and it was likely they knew that the earthquake and its effects were no lucky break. Many of them had probably scoffed in tough-guy language at the notion of gods who were alive. Well, this time there is no mention of giggling or ridicule. Nobody was even moving—not when it was this cozy inside.

STOP, IN THE NAME OF LOVE

At the last possible moment Paul had yelled the words which brought the jailer's thoughts to a screeching halt. With no other motive than love for God and all those who needed to hear the good news about Jesus, the disciples stayed in their dungeon headquarters. Of course, it wasn't a chapel, but it served the same purpose. The fact that Paul and Silas remained, when by our standards they should have been long-gone, is a message to believers today. In sharing the living Jesus with others we're apt to go about it in hit-and-miss fashion.

For instance, we know a neighbor of ours who has never received Jesus as Lord, and we decide it's time (there's a crusade in town this week) to get burdened for him. We drag ourselves from our recliner, reluctantly turn off our favorite program, grab our little-used New Testament, and head for Harvey's place. We knock twice, our stomach does three little flip-flops, and Harvey opens the door, somewhat surprised to see us—actually he didn't expect us to make our regular crusade pitch until the last day of the meeting, as has been our habit for the last seven crusades. Right away we start to make some warm, friendly conversation:

"Say, Harve, ol' buddy. That sure is a nice welcome mat you've got there. Last time I was here it was a little dirtier than that though."

"Yeah, well Bill, you remember you haven't been around since last spring's crusade meeting. It was a wet year."

"Yeah, you know how tied up a guy can get, right? Hey, how's the real estate business comin' along? There's been kind of a housing crunch, they say."

"Gee, I knew people in housing have had quite a time of it, but I suppose real estate is coming along fine. Of course, I wouldn't know. I'm in the teaching profession, but surely you remember that."

"Oh, sure I do, Buddy. Talking about being all tied-up— well, you don't suppose an ol' pal like me could persuade a bosom buddy like yourself to let himself be 'roped' into coming out to our semi-annual crusade, do you? Get it, Harve? Roped?"

"Well, Bill if I could only understand what all this talk about knowing Jesus personally was all about, I might . . ."

"That's okay, Harve. I don't want to put any pressure on a close, personal friend. Don't ever accuse ol' Bill Dogooder of shoving religion down anyone's throat. No siree. Well, I'd better get back home. Can't let those TV's freeze up, can we? Well, I'll surely see you again real soon, Harve. Bye for now. And be sure to say 'hi' to that sweet wife of yours for us." (Bill rushes home just in time to catch a rerun of "Love American Style" while Harve is left bewildered at the doorway, mumbling to himself.)

"Yeah, Bill, see you in another six months or so. And I'd sure say 'hi' to Annie for you, but she died a year and a half ago. Thanks for all your concern. Gee I sure wish I could figure you and your Jesus out. Have a good crusade, . . . Buddy."

If that illustration is as painful to you as it is to me, it's only because there's too much similarity between that kind of "love" and the concern we say we have for people who don't know Jesus. Paul and Silas were not nextdoor neighbors of the jailer. They didn't even take up residence in Philippi—at least not willingly. But out of love for him, they stayed behind to prevent his death and share with him the wonderful words of life.

That's love, the only kind—God's kind. It's the kind of love that sent Jesus from heaven to earth to live as a man. His concern was not his *rights* but our *wrongs:* "Your attitude should be the kind that was shown us by Jesus Christ, who, though he was God, did not demand and cling to his rights as God, but laid aside his mighty power and glory, taking the disguise of a slave and becoming like men. And he humbled himself even further, going so far as actually to die a criminal's death on a cross" (Phil. 2:5–8). He had it all, gave it all, lost it all, won it all back, and has been given by the Father a "name that is above every name."

God's love takes risks, suffers wrong for the sake of getting the good news out, and even dies to make its point. It does not act unbecomingly; it does not seek its own, is not provoked, does not take into account a wrong suffered. God's love is defined in the Scriptures and personified in Jesus who stayed with his Father's will because of his love for us and obedience to his task.

Paul and Silas were not born miracle-workers or some kind of heavenly robots. They were, no doubt, tempted to flee persecution and keep quiet rather than risk beatings, imprisonment, and death in the future. But they, like us, were instructed not to look at the status quo and pout, but to follow Jesus as Lord and shout. Like the writer of Hebrews, they would counsel us to "Keep your eyes on Jesus, our leader and instructor. He was willing to die a shameful death on the cross because of the joy he knew would be his afterwards; and now he sits in the place of honor by the throne of God" (Heb. 12:2).

It's been said that Jesus would have died on the cross to pay the penalty for even one person's sin. The fact is he died for the entire human race. However, Paul and his traveling companion, Silas, knew from experience the value God places on one human being. They had encountered a certain Roman jailer, who, by this time, was finally open to some "good news."

"Where do I sign?"

SEEKING

Trembling with fear, the jailer called for lights and ran to the dungeon and fell down before Paul and Silas. He brought them out and begged them, "Sirs, what must I do to be saved?" (Acts 16:29–30).

The last we heard from the jailer he was preparing to fall on his sword and escape the hands of the Roman authorities, for he assumed that all his prisoners had left after the quake. But Paul became aware of the jailer's suicide attempt and yelled out to him not to do it because all the sheep were still within the fold—not even one prisoner was missing.

Ending his own life was going to be the most difficult thing the jailer had ever done, but now he was sure that above the pounding of his heartbeat he heard a voice. And it sounded like one of the preachers down in the dungeon. Possibly believing the ill treatment Paul and Silas received at his hands had angered their God, this Roman officer was going through a mixture of confusion, relief, and dread terror. He called for someone to bring him lights so he could make his way quickly to the dungeon.

"We're all here," the voice had said. Did it mean that somehow these men or their God was responsible for this happening also? All the other gods were cold, disinterested, and uninvolved in human affairs, but here was a God who wasn't well known in Philippi, and he seemed different. At any moment the jailer probably expected to be wiped out of existence by prisoners, the preachers, or an angry god. Yet why had this God's followers prevented him from running his two-edged sword into his heart? One thing was becoming apparent—that thin ray of light he still called "hope" was waiting for him in the dungeon.

Still in a state of fear and shock, the jailer ran to the cell and fell down before Paul and Silas. The record doesn't indicate how long he remained bowed down in front of them. It was probably long enough for Paul and Silas to reassure him that he didn't need to fear for his physical life because everyone was still inside, they didn't intend to do him harm, and neither did their Lord. Finally the jailer got up and brought them out of their cell.

He'd seen too much simply to put everyone back in their cells, tuck each prisoner in, and go back to bed himself. He'd never seen the fragility of life in this way before. Nor had he ever been thrown face-to-face with his own death. Now he was safe, but the unselfishness and inner calm of Paul and Silas were two qualities he'd never known or seen—not even in battleworn heroes. He didn't know what their God might expect of him, but he was willing to find out: "Sirs, what must I do to be saved?"

LORD, LORD, WHEREFORE ART THOU, LORD?

While God seeks us, places an instinctual knowledge of his reality within us, and initiates the efforts to reach us, it's also true that we must seek him. I used to sit around and try to figure out why God didn't create us with a natural desire to walk around all the time telling the world about Jesus, praying, and singing "Oh Happy Day." Why didn't he force every person everywhere to love him? That sure would have saved everybody a whole lot of trouble—like getting the Bible written, sacrificing all those Old Testament animals, and especially Jesus having to die.

And then I realized that I wouldn't like to be one of several billion strait-laced, expressionless, lifeless robots marching around the world twenty-four hours a day singing "Holy, Holy, Holy." God made us in his image, and that includes the freedom and responsibility of desiring to know and seek him or reject him. It's that kind of awesome freedom—the freedom to choose against Jesus and eternal life after knowing the truth—that began to scare me. So, how does it happen? How do we seek him? How does God operate anyway?

MEANWHILE, BACK IN THE DORM

The same day I realized my glittering plans weren't too neat was the day that marked my beginning as an adult with Jesus as Lord. I had been the center of my little world for so many years that the discovery I wasn't really as all-sufficient as I'd thought I was startled me. Even though the Holy Spirit still lived inside me, I was in a state of spiritual babyhood, and getting *younger* all the time. There were even times when I'd stare off into a starlit sky and wonder if somehow this whole business of God, life, me, and everything else wasn't just a bad dream—one I could never awaken from.

I was sitting in my dorm room gazing out the window, but my thoughts were mostly looking inside myself. I wasn't crying; I was neither high nor low on anything. On the outside it was the best of times for me, but as far as my relationship with God went, it was the worst of times. I certainly wasn't ready to take off for Africa and become a missionary. I hadn't even prayed, honestly talked to God, in months. There I sat, looking at my bookshelf, asking myself a lot of questions: Where was the meaning in life? Education didn't seem to be the cure-all everyone had thought. Why go to school, get married, get a job? If the nihilists were right and everything was absurd anyway, who cares? Why not eat, drink, and be crazy!

Something from within me caused my mind to return to the times when God had seemed close and real to me, especially the time of our first meeting when I was much younger. Then more questions leaped out, demanding answers I wasn't ready to give: What about hypocrites and phonies who claim to be Christians? What about the times you've felt that church was a drag? What about now? Where's God now, Denny? The church has turned off everyone. If Jesus came back and tried to get into one of our churches, they'd kick him out the back door.

Then something my older sister, Pat, once told me came to mind. During the last Christmas break she had given me a New English translation of the New Testament and along with it some sisterly advice. She knew I was struggling, and she said, "Brother, dear. I know you're a real 'cool cat' now and everything, and you might not even read this. But I just want you to know that if you ever really want to find out what this whole deal is all about, read the Gospel of John. End of sermon." I can't tell you how little I appreciated the present or the advice, but she sure spoke my language. When I went back to school at the start of the semester, my present went with me, mostly to satisfy my guilt. Besides, it would be there in case I got bored, and I'd never read a modern translation of the Bible before.

My mind kept coming back to the church. I realized that I had heard, read, and sung a lot about Jesus while growing up in a family who knew him, but who did I think he was now? What had adolescent rebellion and college done to rouse Jesus from his throne? I'd certainly been around and grown up with people who knew and loved him as Lord, but just who did I think he was to me? He's got to be the reason people go to church, I thought. But why, in most churches, is he mentioned so seldom as really being alive, important, central, or even necessary? Why? Where was Jesus?

I decided that if there wasn't really any meat to this Christianity, and if somehow I could come away from his book concluding he was a phony, then life was really a horrible accident or a miserable joke. And I'd been sadly mistaken about "knowing" Jesus earlier in life.

Half afraid that I might find out the awful truth, I did the unthinkable. I grabbed the New Testament my sister had given me and started to read—with an open mind—the Book of John which told about Jesus.

I vowed not to get too involved, and I was careful not to become too interested, but I began reading. I read about a man who claimed to be the Son of God and whose name was Jesus. He made fantastic claims about himself, who he was, and what he could do. He knocked phony religiosity and I said to myself, "Right on!" Religious people who had missed the whole point of loving God, but insisted on keeping long lists of rules, reminded me of much of the Christianity I had seen.

Jesus was different, and all along I had thought he was in favor of stern, solemn, strict, joyless, praiseless "churchianity." I pretended that I would have said those very same things that he said, only I knew he said them much better because they were original with him.

At the end of each chapter I considered laying the book aside, but decided not to stop. I wasn't in a trance or anything; I was just interested. I read the parts where he talked about setting people free, being the only Way, Truth, and Life, offering men life in all its fullness, and telling me that I couldn't even come to him unless the Father drew me to him.

I was beginning to relax. God wasn't going to knock me flat, scare me silly, or buy me off. He respected me and loved me enough to draw me by his gentle Spirit to know him. When I put the book down I had finished the seventeenth chapter and wanted to go on, but didn't. After all, that was quite a bit of Bible reading for a guy who hadn't even had a "word's worth" for ages. Yet I hadn't rolled out of my chair with a skeptic's laughter. This Jesus, whom we paint, powder, and use as an adjective (Jesus-music, Jesus-people, Jesus-jewelry) was definitely a somebody! Now I needed to decide whether or not he would be a Somebody to me.

I wasn't very good at praying. In fact, I was lousy. My best prayers in those days must have sounded like:

> Now I lay me down to sleep, I thank you that I'm not a creep. And if I wake before I die, please take me to your home up high. Sincerely mine, Denny.

At this point I was still unwilling to give my entire life to the Lord. Looking back, I know that I never really believed my doubts about God's existence, the claims of Jesus to me, or my need of him in my life. I just wasn't sure about giving him my whole life. He didn't ask me to be a Sunday Christian. He wasn't interested in five minutes a day with a daily devotional guide. Since he runs it all, my $1.50 a week wasn't going to buy him off either. He wanted me to give him all of me and he would give me himself.

For a long time that afternoon, I had played tug-of-war with the Prince of Peace. For a time I thought I'd concluded that he couldn't have me. But then it struck me that if he couldn't have me, I couldn't have him either. And from what I'd read about Jesus that day, my loss would be the greater. So I talked to him. I was cautious, but honest:

God, did you move? Okay, that is a silly question. I'm the one to blame. Well, God, I want to decide something and mean it. I don't feel like crying. I don't even want to. Sometimes it seems like I've never really gotten to know you at all. I can't promise about years from now, months from now, or even next week. What I'm saying is this: Will you keep getting through to me like you have today? I've goofed it on my own. You gotta help me. Amen.

I want to tell you that he answered that prayer. HAS HE EVER ANSWERED THAT PRAYER! "For I know the plans I have for you, says the Lord. They are plans for good and not for evil, to give you a future and a hope. In those days when you pray, I will listen. You will find me when you seek me, if you look for me in earnest" (Jer. 29:11–13).

"Go, tell it in the dungeon."

SHARING

They replied, "Believe on the Lord Jesus and you will be saved, and your entire household" (Acts 16:31).

The anxious jailer wanted to know how he could find favor with the God of Paul and Silas. No doubt many systems of rigid religion had been the "going thing" in Philippi just as they were all over the empire. Many systems of how-to's, not-so's, this-way's, and that-a-ways exist today as well. All have one thing in common—the answer to how we can be *okay* in God's sight. What effort can we put forth, what creed can we recite, how many quarterlies must we read in order to appease his wrath and convince him of our goodness? In short, "What must *I do* to be saved?"

Few people in Paul's time had to ask him twice to tell them the truth about Jesus being crucified, buried, and risen. In fact, no one. Since their conversions Paul and Silas had searched the Scriptures and were quite able to help a sincere man, woman, boy, or girl to put saving trust in Jesus. This was their calling and their deepest joy in life. Paul and Silas could have gone on all night about the completed prophecies, changed lives, and personal experiences which pointed to a living Lord, but they didn't need to. No one was any more convinced than their jailer friend that this God was a lively one.

Though their reply seems to miss the point of the man's question, that isn't the case at all. They understood what he meant, saw his need, and answered him correctly. He asked "what must I do?," but they answered with "here's who you must trust!" They changed the emphasis from a *what* to *who*. And there was no mistake on their part. Luke records that *they* replied, implying that they both answered him at the same time, with the same solid advice—"Believe on the Lord Jesus and you will be saved, and your entire household." Talk about "one in the Spirit!"

Ready to commit suicide minutes before, the jailer is now at the disposal of a unique God. He wants to do something, go somewhere, risk anything to be saved, and he's told simply to believe on the Lord Jesus. Believing isn't doing, but that was okay with him. He wasn't going to quibble with how God did it. He seriously wanted to be saved God's way. And it seemed that if he would give his heart to Jesus the rest of his family would also turn to him, not because the jailer would force them, but because they would hear the good news, too. And out of it all they got to keep their daddy. Jesus would be alright for them.

"THE TIME HAS COME," THE WALRUS SAID.

In the world which seems dull and routine at times this truth suddenly makes everything come alive again. Every single species and its members are different from other species in some respect. The Bible nowhere teaches a routine mass production of Christians. Each person must come to God for himself at the time when he makes a commitment of his will to Jesus Christ as personal Lord and Savior. Although, for many reasons, it is easier for young people to see and respond to Jesus, there is no magic age at which each person will be ready to trust the Lord. Some churches set up a certain age at which each person learns the doctrines and beliefs of that church and then, at a special ceremony, is received as a member. Other churches without this official policy have an unwritten kind of rule which comes through loud and clear that it's about time to "walk the aisle." And often social and parental pressure rather than the drawing of the Holy Spirit is the deciding factor.

Church membership, though vital and valuable, regrettably does not always assure that every individual has come to the head of the church, Jesus Christ, in personal faith. "You can never please God without faith, without depending on him. Anyone who wants to come to God must believe that there is a God and that he rewards those who sincerely look for him" (Heb. 11:6). In any case, I know frustrated pastors, disappointed parents, and confused converts will welcome the scriptural emphasis not upon what others say we should do, but on what we're actually doing when we make our commitments. And though our decision to join the church or make a public commitment in an evangelistic crusade may please friends, parents, husbands, wives, and pastors, the one each of us must seek to please is God through our own personal faith in Jesus.

OPEN TWENTY-FOUR HOURS A DAY TO SERVE YOU

It didn't really hit me how challenging this whole Philippian episode was until I'd preached about it several times, read it over and over, and tried to put myself into it just a little. Do you realize how difficult it is for most of us to share our faith in Jesus with anyone? We feel so uncomfortable. They feel so uncomfortable. Everybody feels uncomfortable. The right time never seems to come. Somehow the subject of Jesus and his great love just never comes up. His name gets tossed around freely in many places we go, but it is not taken in a serious way. Perhaps we should take a closer look at this situation with Paul, Silas, the jailer, and his family, and hang our excuses out to dry—they're all wet.

It has been a long day for Paul and Silas filled with being dragged across town, whipped by the Romans, and, with empty stomachs, thrown into a cold dungeon. Before they have time to recover an earthquake causes all the prison doors and every chain of every prisoner to fall off. It is now nearly midnight and the keeper of the prison runs into their cell, and falls down before them in fear after they prevented his suicide. Next he escorts them out of their quarters and all of a sudden wants to talk religion—the nerve of that guy!

Paul's philosophy about sharing the powerful news of Jesus was simple. There's no time like the right time, and the right time is now! Speaking the truth in love, Paul and Silas could never be accused of being ashamed of Jesus. The Apostle wrote to the church at Rome: "For I am not ashamed of this Good News about Christ. It is God's powerful method of bringing all who believe it to heaven. This message was preached first to the Jews alone, but now everyone is invited to come to God in this same way" (Rom. 1:16).

Following Paul around the known world was like following a voice crying in the wilderness of a dead civilization. Instead of "prepare ye the way of the Lord," he pleaded with people to "get in on the way of the Lord." Writing later to Timothy, who had been with the apostles on much of the journey, Paul urged the young believer to "preach the Word of God urgently at all times, whenever you get the chance, in season and out, when it is convenient and when it is not. Correct and rebuke your people when they need it, encourage them to do right, and all the time be feeding them patiently with God's Word" (2 Tim. 4:2). So many times in restaurants, at service stations and during my nextdoor neighbor's primetime television viewing, I'm prone to feel that it's the wrong season. The Lord tells me through Paul that there are no off-seasons for sharing Jesus, only off-*reasons* when I'm silent about him.

EVER READY OR NEVER READY

At times I used to wish there were some real good excuses for every believer to hang on to, somehow letting us out of the Bible-prescribed witnessing task we've been saved for. But there isn't one.

"I'm scared," you say. The Bible says, "to stir into flame the strength and boldness that is in you, that entered into you when I laid my hands upon your head and blessed you. For the Holy Spirit, God's gift, does not want you to be afraid of people, but to be wise and strong, and to love them and enjoy being with them. If you will stir up this inner power, you will never be afraid to tell others about our Lord" (2 Tim. 1:6–8a).

"But what would I say? I'm no preacher." The Bible tells us we should begin (and continue) simply like Paul did: "Dear brothers, even when I first came to you I didn't use lofty words and brilliant ideas to tell you God's message. For I decided that I would speak only of Jesus Christ and his death on the cross." There is no excuse for disobeying God's command to know the Scriptures well, even if we don't like to read. "Work hard so God can say to you, 'Well done.' Be a good workman, one who does not need to be ashamed when God examines your work. Know what his Word says and means" (2 Tim. 2:15).

"I know all that is right, but I'm so far behind there's probably no hope with me. God can't use me now." The whole point of being born again is to grow up and become a mature member of God's family, no matter how old we are physically. We don't kill babies just because they can't work algebra problems. God wants you to start where you are right now and grow in him every day. "But grow in spiritual strength and become better acquainted with our Lord and Savior Jesus Christ" (2 Pet. 3:18a), and "long to grow up into the fullness of your salvation; cry for this as a baby cries for his milk" (1 Pet. 2:2, KJV).

Perhaps you see your lack of growth, concern, and sharing with people near you as a sin. Well, don't stew in the juice of your own guilt. Sometimes we think it's more comfortable to live with guilt in several areas of our lives than to bring it all to Jesus and be free and forgiven. He promises believers that "if we confess our sins, he is faithful and just to forgive us our sins, and to cleanse us from all unrighteousness" (1 John 1:9, KJV). These aren't just a bunch of nice words. This is the process by which we can stay on speaking and hearing terms in our spirits with him. Paul and Silas have certainly impressed me throughout this whole incident. But you and I have got to know that the only difference between them and us is Jesus Christ and how much we rely on his power and his love to work within us.

At the start of his ministry Paul could have easily felt depressed and forlorn. Have you ever considered that possibility? If you're like me, you've always thought of the characters of the Bible as having halos over their heads, living way back then in a wonderful forever-and-ever land, and not really knowing what it's like to be real, flesh-and-blood mortals.

Looking back, what the Lord did through the lives of Paul and Silas is truly amazing. But I wonder if they too looked back from time to time at the lives of Old Testament heroes as well—people like Jeremiah, the weeping prophet; or Amos, Ezekiel, and Isaiah? What about Elijah, the guy God just zapped up to be with him? Now that's really living close to the Lord! Just think of Moses and the rod he carried with him. Sure did land those Egyptians in the drink, didn't he? And what about Daniel in the middle of that cage of puddy-tats? He sure was some lion tamer.

Paul could have gone on and on. And if he were prone to compare himself with these men too much, he might have needed conseling before he was through:"Woe is me. I'm only a puny little scholar. What do I know? Sure Gamaliel was my teacher—the best. But here I am stuck in a time of history when nobody cares much about the finest in seminary education. So all I can do is preach. How can God do anything with me anyway? I can't seem to get a congregation and keep it very long. I'll never be another Jeremiah. God probably doesn't love me as much as he did his Old Testament buddies. Why, he walked in the garden with Adam, and David was a man after God's own heart. I'm just sure God goes around in heaven every day singing, 'Small Paul. Small Paul. Small Paul. He's my all.' No chance of that. Sure Jesus is alive and everything. And I guess I had quite a vision not too far back. But they nearly laughed me to tears in Athens. Tentmaking isn't such a bad way to earn a living, I guess. At least everyone doesn't have me pegged as a weirdo."

But that isn't the Paul of the first-century world. Paul was dynamite because, as he put it himself, "I have been crucified with Christ; and I myself no longer live, but Christ lives in me. And the real life I now have within this body is a result of my trusting in the Son of God, who loved me and gave himself for me" (Gal. 2:20).

Paul knew his own weaknesses and was glad for them, because then the power of Jesus could rest on him in a mighty way. Notice the key words in Paul's confident statement, "I can do all things through Christ which strengtheneth me" (Phil. 4:13, KJV). Only when Jesus is number one in our lives are we really happy. Whether we are students, housewives businessmen, retired, or just "tired," we're called upon to share our personal faith with empty people around us.

Milt Hughes, Director of National Student Ministries, in his Share Seminars, advises believers to get into the normal Christian experience by growing as a Christian—getting to know Jesus better and better through daily prayer, Bible study, and regular fellowship. Then introducing someone to Jesus won't be a tacked-on part of our lives but we can naturally share him out of the overflow of a dynamic relationship to him. "Quietly trust yourself to Christ your Lord and if anybody asks why you believe as you do, be ready to tell him, and do it in a gentle and respectful way" (1 Pet. 3:15).

NOTHING DOING

Paul and Silas made it clear immediately that man has no part in God's plan for us to be saved except to receive the "free gift of God . . . eternal life through Jesus Christ our Lord" (Rom. 6:23). Through his death and resurrection Jesus did everything necessary to clear the path for us to be "homeward bound." The huge barrier (our sin) separating us from God's presence was perfectly handled by Jesus. "For God took the sinless Christ and poured into him our sins.

Then, in exchange, he poured God's goodness into us!" (2 Cor. 5:21). "He died under God's judgment against our sins, so that he could rescue us from constant falling into sin and make us his very own people, with cleansed hearts and real enthusiasm for doing kind things for others" (Titus 2:14).

Notice that the real enthusiasm for doing kind things comes after our rescue by Jesus, not before. We cannot earn our salvation; we can only respond to the Savior. For "when the time came for the kindness and love of God our Savior to appear, then he saved us—not because we were good enough to be saved, but because of his kindness and pity—by washing away our sins and giving us the new joy of the indwelling Holy Spirit . . ." (Titus 3:4–5).

The jailer needed to know right from the start who he must trust to save him. He listened keenly as he and his family opened their hearts to God's message. "But God is so rich in mercy; he loved us so much that even though we were spiritually dead and doomed by our sins, he gave us back our lives again when he raised Christ from the dead—only by his undeserved favor have we ever been saved—and lifted us up from the grave into glory along with Christ, where we set with him in the heavenly realms—all because of what Christ Jesus did" (Eph. 2:4–6). This man could certainly identify with the truth about the God who "gave us back our lives again." "And now God can always point to us as examples of how very, very rich his kindness is, as shown in all he has done for us through Jesus Christ" (Eph. 2:7).

JUST JESUS

Jesus died and was judged for our sins, completely paying the price to satisfy God's standards. When we trust completely in him to save us and be our Lord, he enters our lives

and we become God's children. Romans 8:16 says "his Holy
Spirit speaks to us deep in our hearts, and tells us that we
really are God's children."

If we follow Jesus as Lord, our desire will be to serve him
and to respond to what he asks us to do in the world, not in
order to be saved, but because we are saved. "Because of his
kindness you have been saved through trusting Christ. And
even trusting is not of yourselves; it too is a gift from God.
Salvation is not a reward for the good we have done, so none
of us can take any credit for it. It is God himself who has made
us what we are and given us new lives from Christ Jesus; and
long ages ago he planned that we should spend these lives in
helping others" (Eph. 2:8–10). Only trusting Jesus allowed
each individual in the household to be saved. "There is salvation in no one else! Under all heaven there is no other name
for men to call upon to save them" (Acts 4:12).

"I know. I know. There's no doubt about it."

SAVED

Then they told him and all his household the Good News from the Lord. . . . and he and all his family were baptized (Acts 16:32–33).

It doesn't take long for a person to decide to follow Jesus. At this odd hour of the night a Roman jailer and his entire household chose to "call upon the name of the Lord" and be saved. Over a period of about an hour, each individual member heard the "Good News from the Lord," received him willingly into their lives and were baptized by the prisoners. How ironic that two prisoners shared with a jailer and his family how to be set free.

We're not told just where the baptism took place, but it all happened within an hour, so there was plenty of time for the whole, happy congregation to go down to the river and conduct the brief service. There's no reason to think that any other method was used by the disciples than had been given them by their Lord. For the Holy Spirit had baptized them into the Body of Christ (1 Cor. 12:13) and their water baptism would be an outward picture of that inward work. They had been saved.

HIDE IT UNDER A BUSHEL? NO!

I grew up in a situation in which religious language was commonplace. I knew a lot of Bible stories—all about David and Goliath, and the rest of those "rock" stars. But even though I could pronounce almost all of the biblical words, the true meaning of many of them remained a mystery to me—Forgiveness, righteousness, and *Eliot Ness;* substitution, redemption and *multiplication;* justification, propitiation, and *starvation.*

Now, I understood what *starvation* was—that's what occurred in the life of every believer on Sunday morning, waiting for the preacher to finish his sermon so everybody could go out to lunch. And though I thought I had troubles with some of the twenty-shekel words I was hearing, that was nothing compared to the blank look on some of my buddies' faces when I shared my faith with them.

I remember the first time I asked my good friend, Mike, if he had ever been saved. The look he gave me said, "What are you, some kind of nut?" I didn't think he heard me right so I asked him one more time, "Mike, have you ever, in your whole life, been saved? You know saved, s–a–v–e–d?" "Well, I haven't, I don't think, but my little brother has," he replied. "One time when he was a baby he nearly fell out of a window in a tall building and my dad saved him by pulling him back inside. It just about scared everybody to death!"

Of course, that wasn't the kind of "saved" I was talking about, but I didn't know any other words to say so I just kept still. I was worried about his soul, but I figured by that time if I'd told him I was, he'd tell me to mind my own business because he just got a new pair of shoes. After that, for a long period of time I didn't talk to anybody about being saved. It was simply too embarrassing.

IS IT IN THE BIBLE?

One thing I admire about Billy Graham is his unapologetic use of the Scriptures. We're living in a time when "I think," "they voted," "scientists found," "the White House reported," and "Simon says" become rules to live by. No wonder millions are confused. Throughout his ministry Dr. Graham has sounded a clear note—"the Bible says."

No doubt he stays close to the words Paul gave Timothy: "The whole Bible was given to us by inspiration from God and is useful to teach us what is true and to make us realize what is wrong in our lives; it straightens us out and helps us do what is right. It is God's way of making us well prepared at every point, fully equipped to do good to everyone" (2 Tim. 3:16–17). So, everything in the Bible is healing and helpful. Then surely if I'm saved, the Bible can tell me what that means. Then I can share this new life with my friends. Right? I decided to investigate.

The words *save, salvation,* and *Savior* appear nearly three hundred times in the Authorized Version of the Bible. Reading through the Scriptures confirms that this is the main idea God is trying to get across to his people: Man is lost and cut off from God; we can come to God through Jesus and be saved.

Safe really says it. When we're in God's hands by trusting Jesus to be our Lord, that's exactly what we are—safe.

The name *Jesus* actually means "Savior," or "one who saves." In a vision God revealed to Joseph that Mary's baby should be given a special name: "And she will have a Son, and you shall name him Jesus (meaning 'Savior'), for he will save his people from their sins" (Matt. 1:21).

This passage also tells us what we're saved from. Jesus came to save us from our sins—our sinful natures which all of us inherit at birth and display throughout life. One day John the Baptist saw Jesus coming to him, and he said, "Behold the Lamb of God, which taketh away the sin of the world." (John 1:29). Romans 6:23 says, "the wages of sin is death." And Revelation 20:14–15 speaks of a place in which those who reject the Savior must spend eternity without God: "And Death and Hell were thrown into the Lake of Fire. This is the Second Death—the Lake of Fire. And if anyone's name was not found recorded in the Book of Life, he was thrown into the Lake of Fire."

But the earth-shattering message of the gospel news bulletin for all who tune in is that God will pour out his love on us—if we want him to. "God did not send his Son into the world to condemn it, but to save it. There is no eternal doom awaiting those who trust him to save them. But those who don't trust him have already been tried and condemned for not believing in the only Son of God" (John 3:17–18). "Let not your heart be troubled. You are trusting God, now trust in me. There are many homes up there where my Father lives, and I am going to prepare them for your coming. When everything is ready, then I will come and get you, so that you can always be with me where I am. If this weren't so, I would tell you plainly" (John 14:1–3).

First, we're saved from the penalty of sin. Finally, we'll be saved forever from the presence of sin. And with all of this, God's own Spirit enters our lives, making our dead spirits come alive to walk daily in his power.

So, nothing is wrong with "saved" Christians, in fact, they're the only kind. If you're still looking at phonies instead of God's "born from above" kind, cut it out. It'll mess you up. "So stop evaluating Christians by what the world thinks about them or by what they seem to be like on the outside. Once I mistakenly thought of Christ that way, merely as a human being like myself. How differently I feel now! When someone becomes a Christian he becomes a brand new person inside. He is not the same anymore. A new life has begun" (2 Cor. 5:16–17).

There is such a thing as being "saved," Mike. I just didn't know how to tell you before.

ALL IN THE FAMILY

In a matter of minutes an entire Macedonian family began a new life in Jesus. They answered God's call, heard his message, received Jesus as Lord, and responded by being baptized. Now, they were ready to learn how to walk daily as his followers. They were started out right.

Yet, why is it that we do so many things backwards today? Instead of encouraging each other to allow the Holy Spirit to produce his fruit in our lives (Gal. 5:22), we argue over "who's got it," "who can have it," and "what's my gift." Rather than meeting daily for prayer, some of our churches skip the prayer part (or say a token invocaton and benediction) and just meet.

And when it comes to welcoming people into God's family, again the Savior's directions aren't heeded. In Matthew 28:18–20, the Lord makes plain the proper order for entry into his Kingdom: "He told his disciples, 'I have been given all authority in heaven and earth. Therefore go and make

disciples in all nations, baptizing them into the name of the
Father and of the Son and of the Holy Spirit, and then teach
these new disciples to obey all the commands I have given
you; and be sure of this—that I am with you always, even to
the end of the world.' "

Now we can plainly see the sequence: 1) make disciples; 2)
baptize them; and 3) teach these new disciples to obey all the
commands Jesus gave us. But churches of every denomination
have ignored the Master's instructions, or they have reversed
the order, or they have overemphasized one part while
deemphasizing another.

Many churches have rightly seen the task of evangelism as
being the only hope for those who don't know Jesus, the life's
blood of the church. Making disciples by encouraging people
to personally decide for Jesus is vital and scriptural. Only a
living, personal relationship to Jesus Christ can ever save an
individual. But far too many have let the converts stay in their
spiritual nurseries by failing to teach these new disciples to
grow in the faith. Our entrance into our eternal family is by
birth, but babies are supposed to grow. And thousands of
faithful evangelicals are still on the milk.

Some well-meaning churchmen, reacting against this shallow, untaught Christian experience, have gone to the other
extreme. Rather than insisting that individuals make personal
commitments to Jesus as Lord, these leaders have rejected
that approach as "emotionalism" or "interfering with one's
privacy." Instead, they maintain, we should baptize individuals automatically into the community of the local church. This
is then to be followed by an entire lifetime of teaching the
members to "obey all the commands" the Lord has passed on
through his Word.

Yet this approach breaks down also. You can't ask for committed deeds from people with uncommitted lives. But mul-

tiplied thousands of people from these religious traditions are now discovering that they can know Jesus personally. Their lives are changing radically. They're finding that God is alive and his Spirit wants to live and work among them. Many are discovering that, despite the fact that they've been obedient church members and leaders for years and had strong Bible training, they have never actually become disciples of Jesus. Praise the Lord that pastors, denominational workers, and church members, are finding that God's way is the best way of producing mature members of his family.

The jailer and company were now newborn, baptized, disciples, and with the help and prayers of their brothers in the Spirit, they were "ready to grow."

"For Christ himself is our way of peace. He has made peace between us Jews and you Gentiles by making us all one family, breaking down the wall of contempt that used to separate us. By his death he ended the angry resentment between us, caused by the Jewish laws which favored the Jews and excluded the Gentiles, for he died to annul that whole system of Jewish laws. Then he took the two groups that had been opposed to each other and made them parts of himself; thus he fused us together to become one new person, and at last there was peace. As parts of the same body, our anger against each other has disappeared, for both of us have been reconciled to God. And so the feud ended at last at the cross. And he has brought this Good News of peace to you Gentiles who were very far away from him, and to us Jews who were near. Now all of us, whether Jews or Gentiles, may come to God the Father with the Holy Spirit's help because of what Christ has done for us. Now you are no longer strangers to God and foreigners to heaven, but you are members of God's very own family, citizens of God's country, and you belong in God's household with every other Christian. What a foundation you stand on now: the apostles and the prophets; and the cornerstone of the building is Jesus Christ himself! We who believe are carefully joined together with Christ as parts of a beautiful, constantly growing temple for God. And you also are joined with him and with each other by the Spirit, and are part of this dwelling place of God" (Eph. 2:14–22).

"Coffee, Tea, and Me"

SERVING

That same hour he washed their stripes . . . Then he brought them up into his house and set a meal before them. How he and his household rejoiced because all were now believers (Acts 16:33–34).

After being introduced to the risen Jesus and baptized as one of the first members of the church in Philippi, a strange thing came over the jailer. He began to show concern for his prisoners. In fact, even before he was baptized, the jailer was noticing things he'd overlooked before he'd put his faith in Jesus. Paul and Silas had bloody, dirty wounds all across their backs and shoulders as a result of the beating. This would never do. Why hadn't this seemed important to him before?

Here he was with soap and water handy and those to whom he
owed his very life standing near, but their wounds were still
unattended. Right away he personally cleansed the bloodied
backs of Paul and Silas. This must have been very much out of
character for the jailer. But then, that's what Jesus is all about.

After he and his household had been baptized, the entire
group returned to the prison compound. Prison aides had
probably secured the other prisoners by this time, and Paul
and Silas would have to return to their dungeon as well—but
not just yet. This jailer was so full of love and gratitude to
Jesus and his friends that he remembered another need they
surely had. They were probably starving by this time. So it
was well after midnight—big deal! Paul and Silas were hun-
gry. No bread and water would do for his friends, not even a
deluxe TV dinner! I don't know if the jailer did the cooking or
not, but after bringing Paul and Silas up into his own house,
he personally set the meal before them.

It had been quite a day for Mr. and Mrs. Jailer and all the
little "jail-birds." The keeper had been a faithful soldier all his
adult life and in one day everything had changed. He knew it
well. He knew that the risen Lord lived inside him now, too.
In less than an hour his situation had changed from "suicide"
to "satisfied."

I would like to have been sitting around the table that
night. I can even now somehow sense the deep peace, joy,
and newfound love which filled that house. I can picture each
member of the family, still a little bit damp from their midnight service, looking from face to face, unable to hold back
tears mingled unashamedly with laughter. Happy? They had
never known anything like it. But never before had they
known Jesus. Now he was here among them and within them.

"You love him even though you have never seen him;
though not seeing him, you trust him; and even now you are

happy with the inexpressible joy that comes from heaven itself" (1 Pet. 1:8).

Loves Me, Loves Me Not, Loves Me . . .

Whoever said being a Christian is all fun and games? There's just no room at all for floating along on your inner tube down life's rushing river, watching the jagged rocks go by, and "doin' what comes naturally." I know this is true, but every once in a while I have to learn it the hard way: His way works, mine doesn't.

Traveling for several months in close quarters, being involved in intense work, and sleeping too little too often is okay if you're alone, unless the loneliness bugs you. But in our music-evangelism ministry it's different. Multiply the travelers by six or seven, add hundreds of minor and major decisions to be made each week, and prepare for a disagreement now and then. A few months back I don't think I knew a whole lot about the kind of love Jesus makes possible within a fellowship of his people. Everybody on our team had an idea of what it might be like to have a self-giving commitment to each other, but our theory was outstripping our practice.

We had no knock-down, drag-out arguments—nothing that easy to solve. Nor did we have any major doctrinal disputes (nobody suggested that we carry a tank around with us and baptize our followers in Seven-Up). We simply had problems like, "In this song, should we hold this last note out an extra 3, 4, 5, 6, or 7½ beats?" With nearly that number of us, there were times when we held that many opinions. At times the frustrations which existed because we knew we weren't really loving each other supernaturally became too painful. Finally we came to three alternatives.

We could decide that this whole notion of Christian love being something special was a joke, have one more good laugh, and each one of us could run for the four winds. The more we tried to love, the harder it became. As we thought about it, we could see that to say "love is dead" is to agree that "God is dead," and we all knew better than that. We'd been working together with him long enough to kill that idea. Number one was out the window.

The second possibility open to us was to continue ministering together, but pretend that no problem really existed at all. We just wouldn't let anything ever get to a disagreement stage—sort of a see no evil, hear no evil, speak no evil idea. This idea seemed better than the first, but still it left something to be desired— like honesty. Our relationship was very similar to the Soviet-American relationship of the late fifties and early sixties. It was called the "cold war." We were acting like enemies who treat each other and welcome each other for visits like they are friends. Peaceful coexistence might be alright for two opposing world powers, but it would never do for followers of the Lord of love himself.

We had searched the Scriptures. Our concordances were exhausted; so were we. We said we loved each other, didn't we? "Little children, let us stop just saying we love people; let us really love them, and show it by our actions. Then we will know for sure, by our actions, that we are on God's side, and our consciences will be clear, even when we stand before the Lord. But if we have bad consciences and feel that we have done wrong, the Lord will surely feel it even more, for he knows everything we do" (1 John 3:18–29). We were beginning to see that the seriousness of a Christian not loving is comparable to a bank teller passing counterfeit bills to his customers.

As soon as the jailer was saved, he began to serve his Lord by demonstrating genuine love for his brothers in Christ. His changed life was immediate evidence that he'd been born again by God's power. The work he performed now was not to make peace with God. He accepted the fact that Jesus had already completed that job. He helped Paul and Silas because he loved them and shared the Holy Spirit with them. "If we love other Christians it proves that we have been delivered from hell and given eternal life. But a person who doesn't have love for others is headed for eternal death" (1 John 3:14).

That wasn't the jailer's problem anymore—and it wasn't ours either. Millions of Christians, I'm convinced, are pretending that they're really experiencing the "abundant life" Jesus promises, while hiding behind half-baked fellowship and counterfeit love. We weren't pretending any longer, but we needed help.

Our last choice—and the only meaningful one—was to recommit our lives to Jesus and claim his love and power among us in a new way. We had some mountains that needed lowering and a few valleys that only he could fill up. We needed to decrease, so he could increase. We had to die, so he could live through us. The love, power, and presence of his Spirit has remolded us and is daily growing us into a loving family. "For the Scriptures tell us that no one who believes in Christ will ever be disappointed" (Rom. 10:11).

"And the Feet Goes On"

SENT

The police officers reported to the judges, who feared for their lives when they heard Paul and Silas were Roman citizens. So they came to the jail and begged them to go, and brought them out and pled with them to leave the city. Paul and Silas then returned to the home of Lydia where they met with the believers and preached to them once more before leaving town (Acts 16:38–40).

The very next morning the judges sent the local policemen to the jail to have Paul and Silas released. During the night, in fact around midnight, something had occured which made their decision to lock the preachers up a "shakey" one. So the jailer told the pair they were free to go.

But, Paul refused to leave under those circumstances. He and Silas had been beaten publicly without a trial and jailed, and Paul refused to leave secretly. He knew his rights. Paul and Silas were full-fledged citizens of Rome—the judges themselves must come and release them, or they'd simply stage a lock-in. Besides, they had a few friends around the jailhouse now.

When the judges discovered that Paul and Silas were Roman citizens, they started to worry. They might lose their lives over this, not to mention their jobs. The judges, dragging their "tales" behind them, scooted down to the jail and brought the missionaries outside. Then they continued their calm, well-reasoned appeal (they were begging) by asking the pair to leave the city. Paul and Silas obliged, but not without a Philippian follow-up meeting on the way out of town.

The exconvicts made their way to the home of Lydia, who was certainly overjoyed to see them alive and reasonably well. There, with herself, her family, and other Believers (possibly the jailer and his family as well), Paul and Silas preached to them once more before heading south down the coast. The church of Philippi had been born in the lives of these happy people. But even with the Holy Spirit living inside them, these "newborn babes" would need care and prayer. Bidding their brothers and sisters in Jesus a "maranatha" and "God loves you", the disciples left the Macedonian colony and moved south. But Paul would be back once again.

FAITH—IT COMES AND GROWS

The time had come for Paul and Silas to say some words of love and encouragement to the believers gathered at Lydia's place. Knowing the tricks of Satan, the weakness of the old sin nature, and the group's small number, Paul and Silas would choose their words well. They must rely on the Holy Spirit to speak through them to the needs of their "midweek Bible study group."

Leaving new converts must have been especially difficult in the days of the early church. But sometimes it's even harder today. Thousands of churches across the world are Bible-based, capably led by Spirit-controlled pastors, and under girded by mature and dynamic laypeople. This makes it exciting to work in a community which has many such churches where young believers can grow in their walk with Jesus.

However, this is not always the case. A couple of years ago, when a certain young pastor was told about a young girl in his church who had just prayed during a retreat to receive Jesus into her life, he was somewhat stunned. Reminded by her counselor that he had a new believer to help along, the pastor dejectedly commented, "I sure hope I don't blow it."

Lack of proper instruction following a personal commitment to Jesus as Savior and Lord is one of the greatest causes for disappearance among the ranks in churches. Just as babies need a sound diet, adequate shelter, and loving attention, so it is with the spiritual infant. Some new Christians, ignored or discouraged, seem to give up on God, or at least on his Church. And that's bad every time it happens. But the only alternative to evangelism which loses some, is no evangelism at all. The Church is the Body of Christ, and we must win people over to the Good News of Jesus one at a time, and help them grow. Whatever the disciples spoke to the Philippians that day, we know one thing: While Paul warned and scolded his charges at times, he was never lacking for words of encouragement.

"And so, dear brothers, I plead with you to give your bodies to God. Let them be a living sacrifice, holy—the kind he can accept. When you think of what he has done for you, is this too much to ask? Don't copy the behavior and customs of this world, but be a new and different person with a fresh newness in all you do and think. Then you will learn from your own experience how his ways will really satisfy you" (Rom. 12:1–2).

"Keep your eyes open for spiritual danger; stand true to the Lord; act like men; be strong; and whatever you do, do it with kindness and love" (1 Cor. 16:13).

"Always be full of joy in the Lord; I say it again, rejoice! Let everyone see that you are unselfish and considerate in all you do. Remember that the Lord is coming soon. Don't worry about anything; instead, pray about everything; tell God your needs and don't forget to thank him for his answers. If you do this you will experience God's peace, which is far more wonderful than the human mind can understand. His peace will keep your thoughts and your hearts quiet and at rest as you trust in Christ Jesus. And now, brothers, as I close . . . let me say this one more thing: Fix your thoughts on what is true and good and right. Think about things that are pure and lovely and dwell on the fine, good things in others. Think about all you can praise God for and be glad about. Keep putting into practice all you learned from me and saw me doing, and the God of peace will be with you" (Phil. 4:4–9).

"So, my dear brothers, since future victory is sure, be strong and steady, always abounding in the Lord's work, for you know that nothing you do for the Lord is ever wasted as it would be if there were no resurrection" (1 Cor. 15:38).

". . . you are my joy and my reward for my work. My beloved friends, stay true to the Lord" (Phil. 4:1).

Paul and Silas had encouraged the believers. And now, they're off.

"WELL, KING, THIS CASE IS CLOSED."

One of my television heroes as I grew up was Sgt. Preston of the Yukon. Everyday after school, from 4:30 to 5:00, he would go through a "death-defying" adventure just so I could be entertained. Now, that's a swell guy. One of my favorite parts in each episode was when the villains were all tied up, and Sgt. Preston—who had just saved the day—and his lead dog, King, were sitting in front of a warm fire. After narrowly missing death by bullet, spear, and avalanche almost every evening, Preston always looked down at his faithful pal and said the immortal words of confidence and achievement: "Well, King, it looks like this case is closed." Of course it took me years to figure out that it had to close each night because at five o'clock sharp, the Mickey Mouse Club came on.

In spite of new stripes and bruises, Paul and Silas must have felt good inside, knowing that Jesus had seen them through once again. As they moved down the road to the next stop, Amphipolis, I wonder if we could hear Paul reminding himself to take the forward look: "Since we have such a huge crowd of men of faith watching us from the grandstands, let us strip off anything that slows us down or holds us back, and especially those sins that wrap themselves so tightly around our feet and trip us up; and let us run with patience the particular race that God has set before us" (Heb. 12:1). Paul knew that new lives were God's work in the hearts of the Philippians, and he would pray without ceasing for them. But now was the time to be "forgetting the past and looking forward to what lies ahead . . ." (Phil. 3:13b).

It was this kind of righteous readiness which allowed Paul to face death, Satan, and tomorrow with confidence. And writing to Timothy while himself spending his last days in a cell in Rome, Paul could check out of this world to be with Jesus assured that he'd served well: "Stand steady, and don't be afraid of suffering for the Lord. Bring others to Christ. Leave nothing undone that you ought to do. I say this because I won't be around to help you very much longer. My time has almost run out. Very soon now I will be on my way to heaven. I have fought long and hard for my Lord, and though it all I have kept true to him. And now the time has come for me to stop fighting and rest. In heaven a crown is waiting for me which the Lord, the righteous Judge, will give me on that great day of his return. And not just to me, but to all those whose lives show that they are eagerly looking forward to his coming back again" (2 Tim. 4:5–8).

Looking at his own ministry, Paul could say to Jesus with love and humility, "Well, my King of Kings, this case is closed." But for us, it could be a beginning.

A Closing
Introduction

The message of eternal and full life through Jesus doesn't end with Paul and Silas or with the Philippian jailer and his family. It's like a "good news" circle which stretches wide enough and far enough to draw you to trust him. You can give your will to Jesus in a matter of seconds. Does it really make any sense to put it off?

Many people are playing at life, thinking everything will automatically turn out right. On a certain university campus, the score was 34–33 with a minute left to play in an intramural basketball game between the engineering and medical faculties. The engineers grabbed the ball and "froze" it with some fancy passwork. Then the final whistle sounded—and they learned that they were the team with thirty-three points. Please don't quit while you're behind. Trust Jesus now.

1. Admit to God that his diagnosis of your condition is correct.

"Yes, all have sinned; all fall short of God's glorious ideal . . ." (Rom. 3:23).

"For the wages of sin is death, but the free gift of God is eternal life . . ." (Rom. 6:23).

2. Turn from being the boss of your life to having Jesus as Lord.

"For salvation that comes from trusting Christ—which is what we preach—is already within easy reach of each of us; in fact, it is as near as our own hearts and mouths. For if you tell others with your own mouth that Jesus Christ is your Lord, and believe in your own heart that God has raised him from the dead, you will be saved. For it is by believing in his heart that a man becomes right with God; and with his mouth he tells others of his faith, confirming his salvation" (Rom. 10:8–10).

3. Talk to God and tell him your needs and ask him to enter your life. Anyone who calls upon the name of the Lord will be saved. Consider his promise once again:

"For I know the plans I have for you, says the Lord. They are plans for good and not for evil, to give you a future and a hope. In those days when you pray, I will listen. You will find me when you seek me, if you look for me in earnest" (Jer. 29:11–13).

You might want to make this your prayer:

Dear Lord Jesus, I know that I've missed your perfect mark. I have sinned against you and your plan for my life. I've also been the "boss" of my own life. Please forgive me. Thank you for dying on the cross to cover all of my sins. I believe you're alive, so right now I ask you to come into my heart by your Holy Spirit. Thank you for coming into my life and doing all that you promise. Help me to grow in my walk with you and to share my "new life" with others. Thank you for forgiving me and loving me. In Jesus name I ask this. Amen.

If you do pray those thoughts to God and make them your own, God says you are no longer the same: "When someone becomes a Christian he becomes a brand new person inside. He is not the same any more. A new life has begun!" (2 Cor. 5:17).

I'd love to hear from a new brother or sister in Jesus. Please write me soon (Sonshine Circle, P.O. Box 752, Niles, Michigan 49120). I'd like to know of your decision so I can pray for you and write you personally.

If you just now gave your life to Jesus, welcome home. You've waited all your life to follow him. But begin this minute to serve him. Join in the life of announcing to other "prisoners" about freedom in Jesus.